CH

r before

GOLF
CURES
&FIXES

Steve Newell

GOLF CURES & FIXES

foreword by **Ernie Els**

photography by **Angus Murray**

MITCHELL BEAZLEY

Golf Cures and Fixes
Steve Newell

First published in Great Britain in
2007 by Mitchell Beazley,
an imprint of Octopus Publishing Group Ltd,
2–4 Heron Quays, Docklands, London E14 4JP
an Hachette Livre UK Company

Created and produced for Mitchell Beazley
by **Cooling Brown Ltd**

Photographs by Angus Murray

Creative Director Arthur Brown
Editorial Jemima Dunne, Steve Setford
Design Peter Cooling, Tish Jones
Index Hilary Bird

Production for Mitchell Beazley Peter Hunt

A CIP catalogue record for this book is available
from the British Library.

ISBN 13: 978 1 845333 64 5
ISBN 10: 1 8453 3364 0

Typeset in Optima and ITC Officina

Colour reproduction by Sang Choy, Singapore
Printed and bound by Toppan, China

With special thanks to the team at Turnberry Golf Club and the
Colin Montgomerie Links Academy for hosting us and making
available its superb golf courses and facilities for the majority of
photos used in this book; and to Dunston Hall and Northwick
Park for also allowing us the courtesy of its golf courses.
And, of course, thanks to all the models who so generously
gave their time and their expertise to make this book a success:
Chris Brown, Paul Burley, Ricky Hall, and Matthew Naylor
at Turnberry; Stephen Chick at Dunston Hall; Richard Phillips
at Northwick Park; Tiffany Howie and Elaine Ratcliffe.

contents

foreword

Great golf is as much about the bad shots that you don't hit as it is the great shots that you do. But the fact is, we all hit bad shots. That's something you can never eliminate completely from your game. Golf's not like that.

What you can do, though – and I think this is one of the things that really separates the professionals from most amateurs – is recognize the causes of those bad shots so that you can then take steps to correct them. That's how you become a better golfer. It's the same for all of us. We all have to learn from our mistakes.

That's the good thing about this book. It features just about every bad shot in the game, and explains the root causes to help you understand how and why they happen. With that knowledge, and by working on the various practice drills, you can then take steps to try to minimize the number of bad shots you hit.

And as I said before, that's one of the keys to shooting consistently lower scores. I mean, the good weeks that I have are nearly always characterized by a noticeable lack of mistakes. That always feels good!

Steve writes for my website – you might want to check it out at www.ernieels.com. He has also written countless magazine instruction articles for me over the years, and he collaborated with me on both of my books. His knowledge of the golf swing is excellent, so he knows how to analyze mistakes and give advice on putting them right. Hey, to be honest, I've played with him and seen him hit enough bad shots to know he's a bit of an authority on the subject!

No, seriously, he's a good player and, more importantly, he knows his stuff. He's not only worked with me and a lot of the top players in the game, but he's also spent time with the world's best coaches. I think it shows.

This book could be really good for your golf game.

ERNIE ELS

introduction

Whether you are relatively new to the game, a club golfer of many years' standing, or even an accomplished amateur, this book is intended for you. It is written for anyone out there who wants to improve their golf game and shoot consistently lower scores. And that's all of us, right? The better we play, the more we enjoy our golf.

But in order to improve, we need to learn from our mistakes – and I mean that literally. You already have the best coaching aid in the game: your golf ball gives instant feedback on every single shot you hit – good or bad. It never lies or flatters and, as every golf pro will tell you, honest criticism is the first step to improvement. You just need to know how to decipher the messages.

With that in mind, I wanted to show you how to assess every bad shot you make with each club in your bag – driver, fairway metals, irons, wedges, and putter. And I've tried to make it as easy and straightforward as possible for you. Simply find the section on a specific club, then look up the shot that is causing you the problem. There you'll find explanations on how and why a shot can go wrong, what you'll need to do to "fix" it, and "cures" (practice drills if you prefer) to help make those corrections long-lasting.

We'd all like lower scores. I hope this book helps you achieve them. That's why I wrote it.

Steve

STEVE NEWELL

Driver

The slice

This shot is the curse of many a club golfer; indeed, as much as 75 per cent of the world's golfing population is plagued by the slice. You may be on familiar terms with it yourself – too familiar, perhaps! The golf ball begins its flight to the left of the target and curves right in the air, invariably missing the fairway and finishing in the rough on the right-hand side. A modest slice is playable, but it can easily get out of hand, and that's when the major frustration can occur.

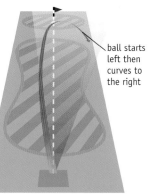

ball starts left then curves to the right

Sliced shot

CAUSE Shoulders "spin-out" in the downswing

X Golfers who slice often take the club back too far inside the line and spin the shoulders from the top.

club is across target line at top of backswing

shoulders spin out, throwing the club outside the ideal line

1

2

The slice often stems from aggressively rotating, or opening, your shoulders too early in the downswing. This throws your hands, arms, and the clubhead outside the ideal line and causes the player to cut across the ball on an out-to-in path. As a result the shot flies left, so over time you instinctively learn to open your clubface in the hitting area, delivering a glancing blow that generates left-to-right spin – hence the slice. The problem is most acute with long clubs such as the driver, because the comparative lack of loft means that there is very little backspin to offset the wicked sidespin.

FIX

Improve the club's pre-hitting position

Instead of rotating your shoulders aggressively at the start of the downswing, you need try let the club drop to hip height *before you start to unwind your upper body*. It might not happen exactly as you plan, but the mere intention helps to slot the club into an improved pre-hitting position, allowing you to deliver the strike from inside the target line. Shots will then start straight. You may for a while still slice or push drives to the right, as it takes some time to get accustomed to *not* having to open the clubface through the hitting area. Let your right hand roll over the left through the hitting area; that will help to return the clubface to a square position at impact.

roll right hand over left, releasing club through impact

keep club on-line for a better shoulder turn

drop club into ideal pre-hitting position

keep head level

club will approach impact on an inside path

1

2

3

✔ From this backswing position it is possible to drop the club into the ideal downswing path and plane, to produce solid contact.

CURE 1

Hit balls with your feet together

This is one of the best training drills to improve a swing. It promotes a better blend of hand-and-arm swing allied to an appropriate body action. Remember, the typical slicer has an over-dominant upper body motion. This drill will get your hands and arms more involved in the action, for the all-round benefit of your game.

stand with your feet together, almost touching

1 Leave the driver in your bag for now, and start with a mid-iron – the 6-iron is ideal. Now stand to the ball with your feet slightly apart; all other aspects of your set-up should be as normal.

✔ The narrow stance forces you to swing the hands and arms more freely, with less interference from the upper body.

make a controlled, three-quarter backswing

keep head level throughout swing

make a free hands-and-arms swing

finish in perfect balance

1

2

3

2 Hit three-quarter shots, making a smooth and controlled swing. Focus on the strike and maintaining good balance. For the time being, distance is not an issue; rhythm and timing most definitely are.

if you apply too
much upper body
to the swing you
will lose balance

3 Once you have hit, say, 20
balls with your feet together
using your 6-iron, reach for the
driver and hit some tee-shots,
only this time from a normal-
width stance. Try to replicate in
your driver swing the methods
you adopted in your 6-iron, feet-
together swings. You should see
a marked improvement in
ball-flight.

"I have always thought that if a game was worth playing at all, it was worth making some effort to play it correctly."

Bobby Jones

THE SLICE

CURE 2

Perform a few rudimentary "pre-flight" routines

It may sound obvious, but you can't ignore the basics with a driver, as its long shaft and relative lack of loft make it very unforgiving.

X If the golf ball is too far forward in your stance, you will find your shoulders and hips are in an open position.

stance width matches shoulder width

ball must be level with the inside of your left heel

weight should favour your right side

60   40

shoulders too open at address

hips too open

arms are too far to the left

toes are parallel to line of target

ball is too far forward

Check your stance: feet should be roughly shoulder-width apart at address, with your weight slightly favouring your right foot.

Check your body alignment: if the golf ball is too far forward in your stance, reaching it will pull your shoulders into an open position so that they are aligned to the left of the target. This in turn causes you to swing to the left through impact. Make the necessary adjustments to your position to cure it.

Push right

This shot can occur with almost any club, but as we're in the driver section I'll deal with the swing traits pertinent to that particular club. I will revisit this topic later in the book (*see p.64*) with other clubs. Basically, when you "push" a drive, the golf ball starts to the right of your target in its initial flight, and then continues in that direction, inevitably missing the target some way to the right. Typically, the trajectory of the ball is a little higher than normal, too.

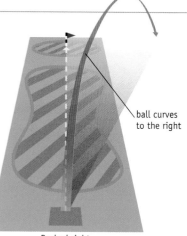

ball curves to the right

Pushed right

CAUSE Trapped in your own downswing

1

hands too low

the club is left behind, trapped on the inside

lower body races ahead in the downswing

2

hands unable to square clubface to ball in time...

...so club travels on exaggerated in-to-out path

ball flies right of target

✗ If the club is trapped too much on the inside on the way down; a "push" is the most likely outcome.

If you're in the habit of hitting a lot of push shots, the likelihood is that the club is getting "trapped" too much inside the ideal downswing plane. Often your legs and hips outrace your hands and arms; essentially you leave the clubhead behind, and it struggles to catch up. As a result, the club is travelling to the right as it meets the ball. If you manage to get the clubface square to that path, the ball will fly straight in the air, but obviously to the right. If your clubface is laid open at impact, which often happens with this swing shape, the ball will start to the right and then curve even further to the right, producing a push-slice. Few golf courses in the world are generous enough to accommodate such wild stroke play.

1

Try to make sure that your hands are more in front of your chest as you swing the club away from the ball...

keep hands in front of chest as club swings back

2

keep club is on line at the top

3

...then look for the same feeling as you start your downswing; this improves the path of the swing, leading to a straighter hit.

hands, arms, club, and body will be better synchronized on downswing

4

club travels on ideal path

FIX

Keep the club in front of you at the start

It is important for you to start working on a shape of swing in which your golf club is more out in front of your body in the downswing – not trapped on the inside, or in essence behind you. Maybe start the process of change by making slow-motion practice swings. Attempt to harmonize your arm swing and body turn, so that everything is working together. It is worth stressing that you should feel as if the club is working more in front of your body as you swing back, down, and through. Try to replicate those feelings in your actual swing. If you rotate your upper body properly then your club will automatically be more "on-line" in the hitting zone.

PUSH RIGHT

CURE

Open your stance and hit shots

Here's a really good practice drill for the range for all those who suffer from a persistent tendency to hit push shots off the tee. It will, with time and effort, gradually help you get your club moving more out in front of your body. As with a previous driving-related drill (*see p.16*), you need to leave the driver in the bag and use a shorter iron to start. This is necessary, as using a shorter club helps to train the correct shape of swing, which can then be incorporated into your driver swing.

(*see p.16*)

1 | **2** | **3**

✔ This drill is perfect for training a more on-line swing; use a mid-iron, then apply the principles to your driver swing.

keep shoulders square

use a three-quarter length backswing

turn shoulder as you swing back

flex your knees

draw left foot back

1 Take something like an 8-iron from your bag, address the ball as normal, then slide your left foot away from the target line. As a rough guide, the toe of your left shoe should be in line with your right heel. As you make this adjustment, try to make sure that you keep your shoulders square. Now hit shots from this exaggerated open stance. Don't make full-out shots yet – just make controlled, 70-per-cent shots. With your left foot drawn back away from the target line, you are encouraging a more active clearing of the left side in your downswing. This helps to get the club more out in front of the body.

2 Repeat several times, or for as long as it takes to get comfortable, then set-up normally and try to replicate those same methods in your swing with your driver. You should find that the club is less inclined to get trapped behind you. Instead, you will deliver it to the back of the ball on the ideal path, sending the ball straight at your target. Wave goodbye to the push!

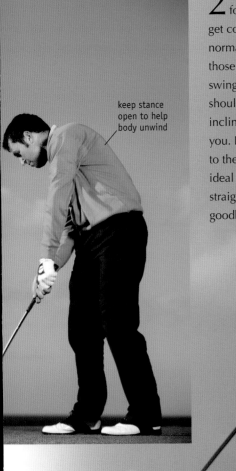

keep stance open to help body unwind

Pull left

With a pulled shot, the golf ball starts left in its initial flight and continues on that path, ultimately finishing left of your intended target. In terms of ball-flight, it is the polar opposite of the push – indeed, if golf were a game solely of driving, then a "pusher" and a "puller" could play the same golf course all day and not get within 100m (100yds) of one another! It should come as no surprise, therefore, to learn that the swing trait of a typical puller is in stark contrast to that of a pusher.

ball curves to the left

Pulled left

CAUSE The dreaded out-to-in swing path

X The club swings on an out-to-in path and the clubface stays square to that path, resulting in a pull left.

club drifted outside line at start of downswing

perfect swing plane

clubface is square to path of swing

ball travels left

target

1

2

The pulled drive is actually a very close relation of the sliced drive: the line of the swing is the same, with the clubhead travelling on a predominantly out-to-in path through the hitting area. Of course, the ball-flight and the end result are anything but the same. The reason for this is down to the position of the clubface at impact. With a sliced drive, your clubface is open to the path of the swing, producing nothing more than a glancing blow that puts sidespin on the ball and causes it to fly on a left-to-right flight path. With a pulled drive, however, the clubface is actually square to the path of the swing, not open. You are, in effect, hitting it flush, which is why shots that are pulled left often travel farther than many other shots.

FIX

Start the ball to the right of your target

It seems an over-simplification to suggest that you cure a tendency to hit shots left simply by endeavouring to start the ball to the right, but that is one of the best ways to remedy a persistent pull. Visualize your ball starting to the right in its initial flight, and try to make that the purpose of your golf swing; the mere intention will help to bring your swing path more into line.

visualize ball starting to right...

... and club slots into a much better position

1

✔ Deliver your club to the ball from inside the line and the pull is history; a powerful draw or straight shot is very much on the cards.

2

CURE 1

Hit shots with a closed stance

Since the swing shape that causes a pulled drive is the opposite of that which results in a push, the ideal practice drill is to close rather than open your stance (*see p.22*). It helps to bring your swing path more into line, gradually moving you away from the tendency to swing the club on an exaggerated out-to-in path.

get club working back on the inside in swingback

ensure shoulders are square at address

draw your right foot away from the target

retrace same path coming down into the ball

1 Take a medium- to short-iron and set-up to the ball as if to hit a regular shot. Slide your right foot back from the target line, so that the toe of your right shoe is approximately in line with your left heel. Make sure that you keep your shoulders square.

2 Hit some practice shots from this exaggerated close stance. You will notice immediate and significant benefits, since it helps you to attack the ball more from the inside, giving your swing a nicely rounded quality.

CURE 2
Remember to check your alignment
With pulled shots – and, indeed, those that are pushed – always have it in mind to check your alignment occasionally. Some supposedly "poor" shots are in fact perfect shots: they only miss the target because your aim is poor, not your golf swing.

keep shoulders parallel to the target line

1 Get into the habit of laying a club on the ground when you practice. That's what the tour pros do, if not all the time then at least regularly. Place the club in line with your toes; it should be parallel to the target line, not pointing at it. Your shoulders and hips should match this alignment. This is what's known as "perfect parallel alignment".

2 Alternatively, ask a friend to stand behind you and observe your set-up. You can't do this in the middle of a competitive round of golf, but it's not a problem during a friendly match.

knees should be parallel to the target line

point club at target

"Place the ball too far back in your stance and you'll probably be aiming right. Place the ball too far forward and your body alignment will be open. Correct ball position encourages correct aim and body alignment."

John Jacobs

Hooked tee-shot

They say that the hook is "the good player's bad shot", but this is scant consolation as your golf ball careers into the trees on the left-hand side of the fairway. The hook shot starts to the right of the target and then once in the air it curves left – often dramatically and depressingly so. It usually misses the fairway and finishes in the rough or, worse, on the left-hand side. Hooked shots also generally travel too low. This is more bad news, given that generating good distance off the tee with a driver requires that you optimize the shot's "air-time".

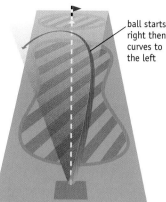

ball starts right then curves to the left

Hooked

HOOKED TEE-SHOT

CAUSE In-to-out swing path and a closed clubface

1

the body has stopped turning in swingback

hands, arms, and club are trapped on the inside

2

position leads to a severe in-to-out swing path

X An exaggerated in-to-out swing path leads to the occasional pull or, as here, if the hands release the club you'll hit big hooks.

In a nutshell, the hooked tee-shot comes about because the path of the golf swing is from the inside. It is by no means the worst of all faults, but in this example it's excessive. The fact that shots are hooking to the left indicates that the clubface is closed to that path the moment the ball is struck. It is this combination of an in-to-out path and a closed clubface that gives you the unwanted hook-spin.

FIX
Try to stay neutral

The cure to your hooking woes is essentially two-fold. First, you need to swing the club into and through impact in an on-line path, not a severe in-to-out path. In that regard, the advice from earlier in this chapter on curing a push will help you (*see p.22*). Secondly, you need to make sure your clubface is square (rather than closed) when it makes contact with the ball. It sounds easy to do, but anyone who has "hooked" for a long time will testify that it isn't. However, with the right advice and some thoughtful application, it is achievable – and probably more quickly than you might imagine.

balance your grasp so that hands, arms, and club are in ideal pre-hitting position

with correct movement, hips will clear out of the way

If your hands, arms, and body work in harmony, your club is more likely to be on the correct path into and through impact.

CURE

Weaken your left-hand hold on the club

If your game is characterized by a persistent hook off the tee, then it is almost certain that your grip is too strong. Any grip change, no matter how subtle, requires patience and perseverance, because initially you will experience some bad times. The fact is, changing your grip is one of the hardest things to do in golf – but ultimately it is the best and most permanent way to turn your game around.

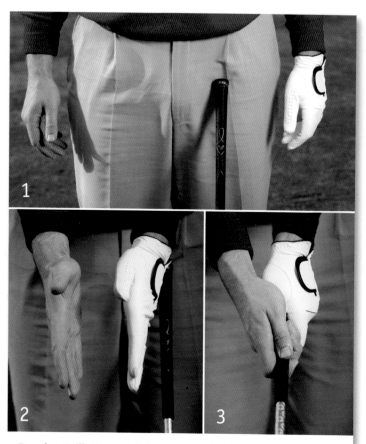

Practice Drill Here's a little routine to help you achieve a more neutral grip on the club. Let your hands hang down by your side, then bring them out in front of you (trying not to twist or turn them either way) in a "clapping", or palms-facing, position. Keeping your hands in this position, put your hands on the club and hold on to it.

1 If your grip is too strong, turn your left hand clockwise on the grip, so that instead of four knuckles, you can see only two, or two-and-a-half at most. Your left thumb should be slightly to the right of the grip as you view it from above.

right shoulder
will be slightly
lower than left

hold club with
neutral grip

hover
clubhead, to
ease tension
in your hands

for driver, ball
must be level
with inside of
left heel

3 Waggle the club back and forth. Make a few practice swings, starting slowly at first, but gradually building up to full speed. Although it may feel strange for a while, this neutral hold automatically works the clubface into a more open position in your backswing.

2 With your left hand positioned, your right hand should then sit more on top of the grip. The "v" formed by your thumb and forefinger should point to your right shoulder. With a hooker's grip, the right hand tends to sit more underneath the shaft.

4 At impact, the clubface will tend to return to a square position – which, of course, is where it started at address. Best of all, you will have achieved this without having had to make any mid-swing adjustments. Soon, you'll be turning those ugly hooks into straight drives!

31

Topped ball

This is a common complaint among golfers at club level and, as the shot is so destructive, it can become a major source of frustration. You may have experienced it yourself – it tends to be a problem with the longer clubs, especially the driver. The ball is struck with the bottom of the club, so it just scuttles along the ground. The good news is the problem is often solved by losing and gaining height in your swing, basically by allowing your head to move up and down.

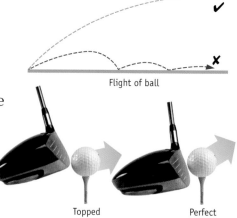

Flight of ball

Topped   Perfect

CAUSE Losing and gaining height in the swing

1

right knee bent at address

2

head lifts in backswing

right knee straightens in backswing

X If you gain height in your backswing, it becomes very difficult to find the correct downswing plane.

Topping the ball occurs mainly because golfers swing the club way past the limit of their body rotation. So instead of finishing the backswing by completing the shoulder turn, the whole body lifts up, the right knee straightens, and the hips over-rotate. Lack of flexibility is often an issue, but whatever the cause, once you lose your spine angle it's very difficult to find the ideal downswing plane. So difficult, in fact, that you might barely make contact with the ball. The clubhead makes contact with the ball above its equator.

FIX 1

Establish good height ...

The key point is to focus on maintaining your spine angle all the way to the top of your backswing. You can use a three-quarter backswing (*far right*) provided you achieve good rotation, and the proper wrist hinge.

1 correct spine angle

2 spine angle hardly changes — head stays level during backswing

✔ This is much better – a three-quarter-length backswing in which the head stays at the same height as established at address.

maintain your spine angle

3 ... and then maintain it!

By keeping your spine angle constant, you don't have to make adjustments in your downswing. You just unwind your body and let it rip through impact – a much better recipe for solid ball-striking.

✔ Maintain spine angle throughout downswing to help guarantee a solid strike and strong ball-flight.

CURE

The height of good swinging

Here's a simple drill that you can practise – either on the golf course or at the driving range, or even in the garden at home in front of the patio doors. It will help you to grasp the feeling of maintaining your height in the swing, thus eliminating that ugly topped drive.

keep chin up

1 Select a driver and assume your normal posture, with your chin up to make room for a full shoulder turn.

keep head level throughout swing

swing freely

2 Now go ahead and make free-flowing practice swings. Your goal is to try to maintain exactly the same head height and spine angle that you established at address all the way through the hitting zone.

bring your
head up

straighten
your spine

3 Follow though after impact. Beyond this point,
your head comes up and your spine angle
straightens, in response to the swinging motion of
the hands and arms. As long as this doesn't happen
before impact, you'll be fine.

"The turning of the hips
to the left initiates the
downswing; the hips are
the pivotal element."

Ben Hogan

Skied drive

This shot is a high entry in the chart of embarrassing golf shots, as any offending golfers will surely testify. It happens because you strike the golf ball with the top-edge of your driver, rather than the clubface. This causes a high-flying shot that resembles something you might hit with a sand-iron, consequently, very little distance is achieved.

As you are using your driver, you can safely say that this is not a good outcome.

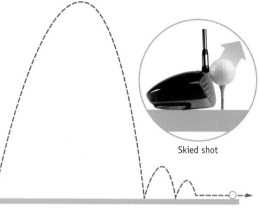

Skied shot

Flight of ball

CAUSE Out of control

1

hands and arms lift the club upwards too steeply

poor shoulder turn

2

X Hitting a skied drive usually has nothing to do with the ball being teed too high; and everything to do with the shape of your swing.

too much body action – almost a lunge at the ball

club comes down too steeply into impact

3

swing totally lacks control

Often, wild shots like this are the result not so much of a specific swing fault, but rather an erratic and out-of-control golf swing. In a nutshell, skied shots usually stem from a total loss of rhythm. Perhaps that is why they are so utterly embarrassing: a fast and furious flurry of effort produces a weak, high lob, straight up toward the heavens. In addition, if there's a strong headwind, you could almost run forward and catch the golf ball! Not the sort of trick you want to be performing, really.

FIX

Find your own sweet rhythm

Putting aside any particular swing flaws, the key to not hitting the skied drive is to really tone things down and start to swing more within your own physical limitations, rather than way beyond them. At address, hover the club behind the ball; this helps to ease tension and keep things more relaxed. Then commit to swinging your club smoothly away from the ball. Try to maintain that smooth rhythm throughout, hitting at what feels like no more than 80 per cent of full power. You should find that you start to strike the ball more consistently with the middle of the clubface, rather than the top edge.

follow the flight of the ball with eyes

hovering your club at address

follow through so clubshaft is across back of neck

make sure belly button faces target

club is in the correct slot at top of backswing

shoulder turns with swing

swing hands and arms down...

...so that body does not lunge at the ball

1

2

Reality check

If ever you lose your balance, you are swinging too hard. That's your signal to tone it down some more.

SKIED DRIVE

CURE

A soft hold promotes a smoother rhythm

One sure way to introduce a smoother rhythm and tempo into your swing is to grip the club more softly. I touched upon this point earlier in the book and, while it may seem a relatively modest adjustment, it has far more significant benefits than you might think. The lack of tension spreads from your hands up into your arms and shoulders. That "softness" in your muscles promotes smoother movements in your swing, whereas, at the other end of the scale, a tight grip creates tension that leads to sudden and abrupt movements and consequently a total lack of rhythm. One of the all-time legends of the game, Sam Snead, was a great advocate of the merits of a soft hold on the club. And he had the sweetest, most enduring rhythm of any golfer who ever played this difficult game. To emulate the great man and bring back some rhythm into your game, try this quick test.

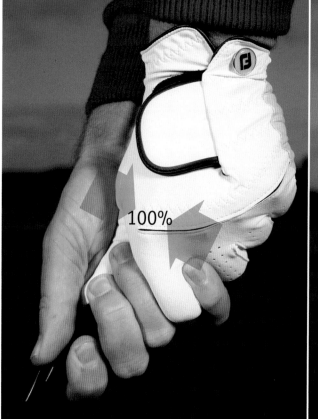

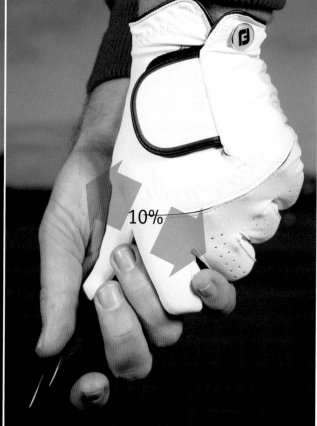

1 Take your driver. Grip the club at what feels like 100 per cent – literally squeeze it as tight as you physically can with both hands. Hold it for at least ten seconds.

2 Next, immediately relax your grip pressure to ten per cent, or as soft as you can without actually letting go of the club. Again, hold for ten seconds.

"Trying to hit the ball as
hard as you can is bull****!
I played at 85 per cent.
Golf is rhythm and timing."

Sam Snead

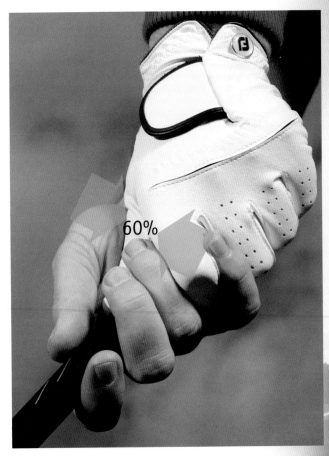

60%

3 Finally, try to split the difference, and you should achieve the perfect grip-pressure for your golf swing. Now swing, but keep it smooth.

Use all of the teeing area

Here is a simple course management idea, adopted by some of the best players in the world. It would be foolish to not follow suit! It's all about increasing your margin for error off the tee, so that you can hit more fairways. The theory is this; if you tee up in the middle of the teeing area and just aim "anywhere down the middle" you have only to deviate either side of that by a margin equivalent to half the width of the fairway and your ball finishes in the rough. However, simply by altering your teeing position and your aim, you can effectively give yourself a bigger fairway to hit.

Everyone has a natural shape of shot. If your tendency is to hit your driver with a draw or hook – in other words, on a right-to-left ball flight – then tee up on the left-hand side of the teeing ground and aim away from the trouble down the left. This way, you have given yourself the luxury of a whole fairway to hit, with a margin for error either side of your chosen shot It's all about playing the percentages; something the pros are rather good at. If your tendency is to hit your driver with a fade or slice – in other words, on a left-to-right ball flight – tee up on the right hand side of the teeing ground and away from the trouble down the right. If the shot goes according to plan, you'll split the middle of the fairway. If it flies too straight, you hit the left side of the fairway and if it fades too much, you hit the right side of the fairway. This gives you not half of the fairway to hit, but the whole fairway.

tee-up left if you draw or hook

SMART GOLF

tee-up right if you fade or slice

Fairway metals

The "sclaff" shot

Messy shot, this one – on a wet day, very messy. In fact, keep this up for long and your dry cleaner will soon become a close personal friend. How come? Well, in the "sclaff" your clubhead makes contact with the ground before the ball, gouging out a huge divot and, in boggy conditions, spraying your entire front side with a cocktail of rain and mud. In addition, the lack of clean contact results in poor ball-flight and catastrophic loss of distance.

Sclaffed shot

CAUSE A race won by your hands and arms

X The trouble here is that your lower body races ahead, hands and arms get left behind, and the club is then released too early.

backswing isn't quite completed...

...before the lower body starts to race into the downswing

body has stopped turning

club is released too early

When you're hitting a lot of shots fat (*see p.76*) – and that is basically what the sclaff is – it is often because your hands and arms are "out-racing" your body and releasing the club too early in the downswing. The club basically bottoms-out before it reaches the golf ball. So, without wishing to get too personal, your body stops turning, and your hands and arms are doing proportionately too much work.

FIX

Get your body back on even terms

What you need to do is redress the balance by synchronizing your downswing motion. Try to feel your body turning through your hands and arms easily, so that everything moves in harmony. The result is that everything arrives at the impact together. That is the essence of good timing.

good balance is a by-product of a well coordinated swing.

unwind your body through impact

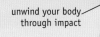

1

2

✔ The key here is to make sure that your lower body unwinds at the same time as your hands and arms deliver the club into the back of the ball.

THE "SCLAFF" SHOT

3

CURE 1

Step on it!

This is what one might describe
as an advanced drill, but it's a very
effective way of conveying a sense
of your legs and hips initiating the
downswing, which is exactly the
medicine you need.

1 Using a 6-iron for now, get
yourself comfortable at address.
As you make your backswing, shift
your weight on to your right side and
let your left foot come off the ground.

set-up as normal for address

lift your left foot off the ground in your backswing

CURE 2

Think rhythm, not distance

With these long clubs, it's easy to
become obsessed with distance. This
isn't a particularly constructive thought
process, regardless of the choice of
club. On the golf course, in the
middle of a round of golf, you need
to be thinking about rhythm instead.

1 Your set-up needs to be the same
as for your driver, with your weight
slightly favouring your right foot and the
ball opposite the inside of your left heel.

balance your weight 60/40 to your right side for long shots

60   40

THE "SCLAFF" SHOT

2 From the top of your backswing, initiate the change of direction by stamping your left foot down on the ground. This causes your weight to shift towards the target first, followed by your hands, arms, and club. Then simply carry on to a balanced finish. Repeat this several times.

3 The decisive move at the start of the downswing gets your arm swing, weight shift, and body action working in harmony. There's no early release, and no horrible sclaff. Just clean, solid contact. Switch to your fairway metal and try to replicate the same feelings in your swing.

stamp left foot to ground to initiate downswing

good weight shift leads to solid strike

sweep your club away low to the ground

make the fullest shoulder turn you comfortably can on upswing

swing smoothly to a balanced finish

2 Think "low and slow" as you take the club away from the ball. When you get to the top of your backswing, make a smooth first move down and try to feel as though you are sweeping the ball away. Don't force it. A sweet strike is what you're looking for. Let the design of the club and its loft produce the distance for you. Trying to force things will only lead to miss-hits and a loss of accuracy – and possibly your golf ball with it!

Heeled ball

The effective "sweet" spot on modern golf clubs, such as the fairway metal, is far bigger than on the clubs of yesteryear. Indeed, an old wooden clubhead had almost no forgiveness whatsoever; thus, anything but a perfectly struck shot would produce very poor shot patterns. Even with the new clubheads, hitting a shot out of the heel with a modern fairway metal produces less-than-satisfactory results – typically a low-flying ball that travels to left of the target and often slices to the right.

ball starts left but drifts right

Flight of ball

CAUSE The reverse pivot

weight too evenly spread

ball too central to stance

weight moved to left, instead of to right reverses pivot

X Ball too far back in the stance is a major cause of heeled shots.

If you are hitting a lot of long shots out of the heel of the fairway-metal clubface, it sounds very much like a case of "reverse pivot". This happens when your weight gets stuck on your left foot in the backswing, and falls back on to your right side in the downswing – the reverse of what should happen in an effective golf swing. Imagine a boxer falling backwards as he tries to punch an opponent – he won't do much damage, will he? Well, that's the effect of the reverse pivot on your golf swing – you'll generate very little power. Compounding the problem, and to certain extent causing it, the ball may not be in the correct position in your stance, here it is too far back, and it's difficult to find the middle of the clubface from there.

FIX

Get behind the ball and sweep it away

Position yourself so that the ball is further up in your stance, opposite the inside of your left heel. That is the first corrective measure. It will help you to get behind the ball at address – a head start, as it were, for what you are trying to achieve in the swing. From there, you need to let your weight follow the direction of the swinging clubhead – let it flow on to your right foot in the backswing, transferring it on to the left side in the downswing and through impact. In other words, the reverse of the reverse pivot! Now you'll start to "punch your weight".

weight should slightly favour right side

ideal ball position for a fairway metal shot

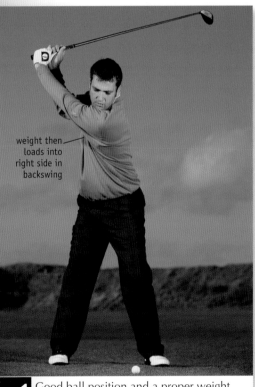

weight then loads into right side in backswing

✔ Good ball position and a proper weight shift results in solid contact.

CURE

Think "turn and point"

The advice on the previous page is designed to help improve the overall shape of your golf swing. The main aim is to eliminate the tendency to reverse pivot, enabling you to sweep the ball away with perfect, flush contact. The "turn and point" practice drill below builds on this advice, and gives you something to work on between games.

✔ Turn your back on the target and try to point the club-shaft at the target at the top. Simple idea; great result.

wrists are hinged correctly

back should face the target at the top of the swing

1 Set-up to the ball, with good alignment, using your favourite fairway metal.

2 In the backswing, concentrate on "turning your back on the target", while at the same time transferring your weight onto your right side.

3 As you get to the top of the backswing, try to point the club-shaft straight down the target line.

4 Concentrate on shifting your weight on to your left side as you swing down and through. The improved weight shift, combined with a free hand-and-arm swing, will give you a better angle of attack. It's quite a contrast from the reverse pivot – and your ball-flight will reflect that.

Lack of power

This can be an extremely frustrating affliction, for in many ways you may feel that contact is out of the middle of your clubface. Yet the results do not reflect that, in as much as the ball travels nowhere near the distance you'd expect given your performance with the more lofted clubs in your bag. Indeed, you may fly your 5-iron farther through the air than your fairway metal, which is very frustrating. In doing so you will miss out on all the benefits of this versatile club.

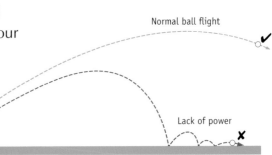

Normal ball flight

Lack of power

CAUSE No "zip" in the swing

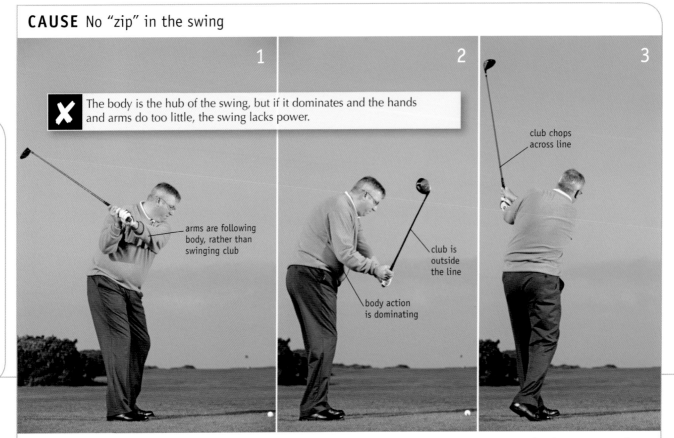

X The body is the hub of the swing, but if it dominates and the hands and arms do too little, the swing lacks power.

1

arms are following body, rather than swinging club

2

club is outside the line

body action is dominating

3

club chops across line

With the more generic shot problems such as this, there are obviously many possible causes. However, the most likely explanation is that you are moving the club on a predominantly out-to-in swing path, characterized by excessive upper-body motion and an ineffectual hand action. The resulting weak impact conditions lead to a strike that lacks, for want of a better word, "zip"; there's just no real power.

FIX

Turn the tables

Your body still needs to play a major part in the action – it is, after all, the engine room of your golf swing. But your swing needs to be a more dynamic movement, combined with the appropriate hand-and-arm action. In short, you need to feel that your hands and arms swing in response to the turning motion of the body, not the other way around.

initiate swing with body turn

hands and arms swing club into full finish

finish with body facing target

✔ Your body should be at the hub of the swing, with your hands and arms working in harmony to develop power at impact.

feel your body work in unison with hand-and-arm action

raised right toe indicates good weight shift and rotation

1

2

3

CURE

Learn to move into the ball

This drill works wonders if you lack power in the swing; it gets you moving into the golf ball with a positive weight shift and good extension through the ball, to help maximize the power in your golf swing.

set up as normal

tee-up second ball ahead

knock away the first ball

1 Using your driver, address one ball in line with your left heel and tee-up a second ball 15cm (6ins) or so ahead of it.

2 Now, just knock the first ball away but keep the clubhead where it is, still 15cm (6ins) behind the other golf ball.

focus on
teed-up ball

get behind the
ball with a good
shoulder turn

✔ The key to this drill is to learn to shift your weight purposefully
to your left side and really chase after that second ball!

3 Swing and try to hit the second
ball. It may seem strange at first:
you'll feel that you're having to
"reach" for it a little bit, but consider
that a positive sign. It will get your
weight moving in harmony with the
swinging clubhead. Soon your club-
release will be better and you'll
achieve good extension through the
ball, which is great for your striking.

3

Play a smart lay-up shot

There is obviously much we can all learn
from the world's top players. This applies
not only to technique, but also to course
management. The fact is, tour professionals
think "smarter" than the average club golfer.
The lay-up is a classic example – one where
you can take a leaf out of the pros' book
and save shots in your game.

The situation is relevant on par-5s and
long par-4s, where holes are out of reach
either as a result of a poor tee-shot or simply
by virtue of distance. Basically, if you can't
hit a green with this shot, make your next
shot as easy as possible. Think carefully.
What is your favourite pitching distance?
Tryto place your lay-up shot into that "zone"
with a fairway metal. Don't go all out for
maximum distance, because being closer
to the green doesn't necessarily mean you're
faced with an easier shot; in fact it's often
quite the opposite.

When the green is out of reach, most tour pros
typically leave themselves a favourite pitching
distance – say, 70–80m (80–90yds), which is the
ideal range for a comfortable swing with a lob-
wedge. That way, the player has maximum control
of the trajectory, distance, and spin; all the
ingredients of a successful pitch shot.

pitch shot to green

pitching zone for lay-up shots

Long irons

Poor carry

Let's establish a few hard facts before travelling too far down the long-iron road. These are probably the most difficult clubs to use in the whole game of golf; even some of the best players in the world have swapped their longest irons for the equivalent lofted wood. So if your long-iron shots lack power and you aren't – as the title indicates – able to carry the ball a decent distance through the air, well, join the club. You're one of many. That doesn't mean it isn't frustrating, however, there are solutions.

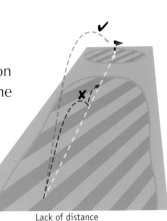

Lack of distance

CAUSE Physical ability

> ✕ The tendency with long-irons is to try to help the ball into the air. In practice it never works.

poor wrist hinge

no body turn

1

weak strike

weight stuck on right side

2

Poor carry can be a physical problem, as well as a technical one. The truth is (and it seems harsh), a lot of golfers aren't able to generate the necessary clubhead speed to make long-irons work. You simply might not be strong enough or flexible enough to use these clubs

effectively. There's no shame in it. You just need to clarify your own position on this. Is your problem a physical one, in which case you need to look for other options, such as better club selection? Or is it merely a straightforward mechanical flaw, which is fixable?

FIX

Facing the fundamentals

Let's first assume you are more than capable, physically speaking, of hitting with a long iron. In which case, check your set-up. The ball needs to be just inside opposite your left heel (or a ball's-width further back if you prefer). Make sure your hands are working properly, with good wrist-hinge in your backswing, and that you are flexible enough to make a proper (effective) shoulder turn. These are fundamental requirements for any golfer wanting to hit solid long-iron shots. In addition, the various parts of your swing need to be perfectly "connected" in order to exert some authority over your long-iron play.

If you feel that long-irons are best left in your golfing past, then a hybrid club is what you need. This is described later in this chapter (see p.72).

hinge wrists properly

1

2

wrists fully set

turn body in swing

3

result is powerful strike

4

✔ You must let your weight flow in the direction of the swinging clubhead to achieve powerful ball-striking.

5

CURE

Maintain the width in your swing

You need to focus on improving your technique so that you can regain some of your long-iron prowess and start using these clubs again – rather than just carrying them around as "excess baggage" in your golf bag. Think of the key term "connected", which I described on page 61. This "connection" helps you to maintain the width of your swing and promotes an effective application of the clubhead to the ball. It ensures that whatever clubhead speed you generate is *effective* clubhead speed. Here's a useful practice drill to include in your long-iron practice sessions.

✔ Make sure you sweep your club away "low and slow", and keep your prop (here we've used a basket) in place.

trap a basket between your elbows

keep a basket in place during your takeaway

1 Address the ball using a long-iron and trap a ball basket, or small soccer ball, between your elbows.

2 Now make a backswing while "squeezing" the object between your elbows to stop it falling to the ground.

3 Squeezing the basket between your elbows "connects" your arm swing to your body turn, and thus introduces a wide arc to your golf swing. As you complete your backswing, let the basket fall to the ground, its job done. Rehearse this a few times with your object, then try to repeat the same movement without it – only this time go ahead and hit a golf shot.

keep arm swing
in sync with
body turn

let basket
fall as you
complete
backswing

hands release
club through
the ball

4 You should find that the width you introduced at the start stays with you throughout the rest of your swing, to the benefit of your long-iron play.

POOR CARRY

63

The push-slice

Although there are far worse shots than this, the push-slice is nevertheless irritating. The golf ball starts down the right-hand side of the fairway and either stays right, or tends to slice to the right in mid-flight – often on a higher-than-anticipated trajectory. No matter what you do, you can't seem to straighten out that ball-flight.

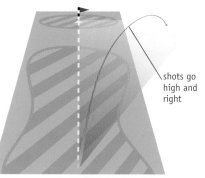

shots go high and right

Push slice

CAUSE Lack of load

lack of load causes weight to move on to left side...

...then on to right side in follow through

X The reverse pivot is one of the most destructive faults; there is no way you can hit good shots from here.

1

2

Once again, it is worth stressing the fact that the long-iron is an uncompromising beast: it magnifies the slightest flaw in your swing, causing you to produce disproportionately bad golf shots. The long-iron can make you feel like you're swinging the club even more

than you actually are. In reality, the problem could be nothing more serious than a case of not loading your weight properly in your backswing, which leaves you forever struggling to generate the kind of clubhead speed that long-irons thrive on.

FIX

The need for speed

The solution is simple, although not so easy to achieve. You basically have to generate a bit more speed through the hitting area. This, quite rightly, has been a consistent theme throughout the long-iron section. Learning to make a more powerful turn and loading your weight more efficiently will go a long way towards enabling you to hit with some conviction using this most demanding of clubs.

body turns through downswing...

...as hands and arms deliver the strike

make a full shoulder turn in backswing

weight should be to right in backswing

begin to shift weight right-to-left in downswing

✔ Here the weight moves to the right in the backswing, and to the left in the downswing; much better!

THE PUSH-SLICE

CURE

Get your left shoulder over your right knee

This drill works best if you rehearse it in between hitting shots at the range, so that you gradually instil the correct moves into your proper swing.

1 Grip your club as normal using a long-iron. Then take your right hand off the grip and clasp it around your left wrist.

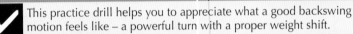

This practice drill helps you to appreciate what a good backswing motion feels like – a powerful turn with a proper weight shift.

grip left wrist

pull arm straight back

be aware of position of left shoulder

finish with left shoulder over right knee

2 Use your right hand to add extra momentum to your backswing movement, literally pull your left arm and the club away from the ball. Use this momentum to really stretch your upper body into a full turn. You're aiming to have your left shoulder finishing over your right knee at the top of the backswing. This indicates that you have acheived a full turn and a good weight shift. Some coaches will refer to this as "loading" your weight on to your right side.

Top-edge strikes

The long-iron tee-shot is a good strategy to adopt on short par-4s, where accuracy is at a premium and maximum distance is not an issue. But without proper execution, it can all go horribly wrong, leaving you perhaps out of range of the green in two or, at the very least, facing another long-iron shot. A common problem that many golfers experience when trying to hit a long-iron shot off a tee-peg is that they strike the golf ball with the top-edge of the clubface, which produces weak shots that travel only a short distance.

Top-edge strike

CAUSE One scoop too many

✗ If the ball is teed too high and your weight shift is wrong, a poor strike is inevitable.

1

2

3

Top-edging the ball often occurs because a golfer wants to help the ball into the air, which itself stems from a lack of confidence. The long-iron looks as though it possesses even less loft than it actually does, and it can be hard to resist trying to lend a helping hand. Some golfers tend to tee the ball too high, assuming that this will help. It doesn't, it merely exacerbates the problem. In addition if they try to add even more loft through impact, which means that they tend to lean back on to the right side and scoop at the ball. The net result is a weak, upward strike, often out of the top-edge of the club.

FIX

Signal your intentions with the shape of your set-up

Forget about helping the ball into the air. Remember the old saying, that you have to hit down on the ball in order to get it to travel upwards. Your address position should reflect that. Tee the ball down. The ball should be just forward of centre, with your hands ahead of the ball, and the shaft and your left arm forming a straight line down to the golf ball. Make a full turn, remembering the phrase we refered to above, and get behind the ball. This requires you to shift your weight on to your right side in your backswing, followed by a purposeful weight shift on to your left side in your downswing.

good posture at address is essential

set ball in ideal position

make full turn in backswing

keep right knee flexed

move weight to left side at start of downswing

1

2

3

 Ball is teed down, well placed in stance, and weight shift is good: a proper strike is on the cards here.

CURE

Try to hit Tiger's famous "stinger shot"

Long-irons are difficult to use. This is partly due to their lack of loft, but also to the length of the shaft. You can overcome the difficulties of a longer shaft by choking down on the grip, which can make the club feel more like a 5- or 6-iron, and thus a lot more manageable.

Also, you might want to practise hitting Tiger's famous "stinger", which is essentially a full-punch shot, where the ball takes off low and flies like a bullet at its target. You obviously won't be able to hit it quite like Tiger does, but the intention to do so will give your swing some useful characteristics that can improve your long-iron play.

To hit this powerful stinger shot, you need to "feel" how your upper body "covers" the ball at impact.

weight shift on downswing

keep hands forward

1 Your set-up is crucial. Check it in a mirror or ask a friend to watch you. The ball should be 7–10 cm (3–4 ins) inside your left heel, and your hands should be in front of the golf ball.

2 Make what feels like a compact backswing. Keep the shaft of your club short of horizontal at the top, but still make a full-shoulder turn and load your weight into a flexed right knee. Don't snatch the club down. Just make a smooth transition.

3 Then pour on the power; keep your hands and arms swinging in harmony, with a good weight-shift on to your right foot. Commit yourself fully to the strike and feel yourself staying down through the shot. You don't need to make a conscious effort to hit down steeply into the back of the ball – the correct address position effectively pre-sets that. Just try to feel that your chest "covers" the ball as you swing your club through the hitting area.

 Really drive your hands low through the ball, punching it down the fairway.

Hybrid clubs

I like to think you're able to play this shot with a 2- or 3-iron, but realistically you might find those clubs a bit unforgiving. In which case, switch to a hybrid club or driving iron. The same technique applies.

Help is at hand from a hybrid

Two decades ago, all tour pros worth their salt carried a 1-iron in their bag. Nowadays, there probably isn't a single golfer in the world's top-200 who has one. Indeed, many now don't even carry a 2-iron. These clubs have been relegated to the cupboard under the stairs and replaced by one of the new breed of hybrids. A hybrid is an ingenious club that combines the distance of a long-iron with the ease of use of a mid-iron. They are, quite simply, brilliant.

The secret to the success of the hybrid lies in the design of the clubhead. With an iron there is only so much the manufacturer can do in terms of distributing the weight around the clubhead to make it forgiving to off-centre strikes. But the more rounded, comparatively chunky hybrid design offers greater potential to redistribute the mass of the clubhead so that it boosts the size of the sweet spot and, crucially, lowers the centre of gravity. This increases the launch angle, enabling you to get your ball airborne more easily. A hybrid doesn't demand a super-fast clubhead speed to do its job, either. High-flighted long shots are back on the agenda!

For placement shots off the tee, or shots into long par-3s such as this, the hybrid is ideal. It is easy to hit and generates acceptable distance. Equally, for long fairway shots on to greens they are a great weapon, producing a ball-flight much higher than that of the equivalent long-iron, which enables you to hold the green.

Mid irons

The fat shot

This is a shot in which the clubhead hits the ground before it makes contact with the ball. A fat shot can occur with varying degrees of severity. Pros will hit some shots fat during the course of every tournament, but only marginally, so it can be difficult to detect. The ball will probably come down maybe 6–9m (20–30ft) away from where they intended, which doesn't usually ring any alarm bells with the public. But when an amateur hits a shot fat, it tends to be pretty obvious. In extreme cases, the divot sometimes travels almost as far as the golf ball. At the very least, a fat shot will travel barely a fraction of the required distance.

Hitting the ball "fat"

CAUSE Body shutdown

club is released too early

X If you stop turning your body through the downswing, it is very easy to hit a shot fat.

club bottoms out before it reaches the ball

1

2

More often than not, a fat shot is the result of your body "going to sleep" mid-swing. For some reason, your shoulders and torso don't move properly. It may be a fault that you have drifted into over a long period of time, and it may not always be evident. But when it happens, maybe towards the end of a round when you're starting to feel a bit tired, it makes it very difficult for your hands and arms to deliver your club cleanly to the back of the ball, or indeed release it freely through to the target. When this happens a fat shot is the most likely outcome, although golfers will occasionally hit shots "thin", too.

"bump" hips to your left, when initiating downswing

turn body as hands and arms swing

1

2

Make practice swings in which you concentrate on ensuring that your hands, arms, and body are all working together.

FIX

Think of the golf swing as "two turns and a swish"

In order to cure yourself of this particular swing flaw you have to give your body a wake-up call. A really good way to achieve this is to start thinking of your golf swing as "two turns and a swish". Try to make that your overriding thought both in your practice swing and in your actual swing. Turn to the right in your backswing and "swing" your arms to the top, then turn to the left in your downswing and "swish" the club through the hitting area with a lively hand-and-arm swing. *Two turns and a swish* – it's the golf swing in its purest form.

keep body turning all the way through the swing

3

CURE

Practice baseball swings

This is another of those wonderful practice drills that can be rehearsed either at the range between shots, or on the golf course as a mid-round reminder to help maintain the correct shape to your swing. You can even do it at home, perhaps with a weighted golf club, to train the body when you don't have an opportunity to play a lot of golf. The benefits are significant; it promotes the feeling of your swing being "two turns and a swish".

1 Stand upright with your hands and arms out in front of you, and the club just below shoulder height. Take baseball-style swings, making a full turn back and through as the club swings freely around your body. Start slowly, then build-up speed and try to make the clubhead swish as you swing through the hitting zone. Then bend over ever-so-slightly from the hips, lowering hands to just above your waist. Repeat the exercise.

hands at shoulder height

2

3

1

 Turn your body and make a free "swish" of the club. Feel the speed of the club at the point where the ball would normally be.

✔ With each practice swing, lower your club a little closer to the ground, but work on retaining the same feeling of freedom.

lower hands to hip height

turn and "swish"

2 Bending from your hips, now lower the club so that your hands are level with your hips. Repeat the exercise, focusing again on the rotary motion of your upper body. You should find that your hands and arms respond to that rotary motion, swinging in harmony around your body.

adopt normal posture

turn to the top

swing freely through

3 Finally, adopt your normal golfing posture, with the club resting on the ground. Try to recapture the feelings you had in your "baseball" swing, and then incorporate them into your actual practice swing.

THE FAT SHOT

Rough trouble

It is a marvel how well the leading pros hit shots from even the deepest rough. Where one would assume escape was the only option, they somehow generate enough power to bomb the ball on to the green 165m (180yds) away. Try as they might, however, most amateurs cannot achieve anything like the same distance from rough as they can from the middle of the fairway with the same club. The strike is typically poor, and the golf ball comes down way short of the target.

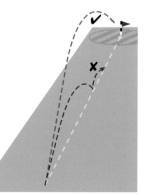

Lack of distance

CAUSE Too shallow into the ball

ball too far forward in stance

X Incorrect set up from the start can create poor, often shallow, angle of attack, which won't get you out of the rough.

1

2

Good rough play is not all about power. It is more about generating the correct, descending angle of attack, and that is what is usually lacking when you struggle from the rough. By far the most common problem is a shallow angle of attack, which works when you're hitting a driver off a tee-peg, but it's hopeless when the ball is sitting down in rough. Too much grass gets trapped between the club and the ball, which effectively cushions the blow. Hence the distance is so drastically reduced.

FIX

Train a steep angle of attack

To hit good, solid golf shots from the rough you have to generate a steep angle of attack into impact. Without that, all the muscle power in the world isn't going to help you one little bit. So, start by putting the ball back in your stance. This is crucial. Anything forward of central won't work. From here you will find it easier to hit forcefully down into the back of the ball, the steeper angle of approach ensures that less grass is trapped between the clubface and the ball. In effect, you're generating a cleaner strike, and both distance and ball-flight will improve as a result.

use hands to lead club into ball

keep hands forward

ensure good wrist hinge

1

2

✔ Your set-up is crucial when you are stuck in the rough; think "ball back, hands and weight forward".

keep a steep angle of attack

3

CURE

Try the tee-peg check

To hit good shots from rough it's essential that you set your club properly in your backswing, with the appropriate wrist hinge, as this helps to promote that all-important steep angle of attack. Here's a practice drill to help ingrain that into your swing.

1 Place a tee-peg in the butt-end of the grip on, say, your 7-iron. Go into the rough, place the ball in a pretty poor lie, and organize your set-up so that the ball is in the middle of your stance.

✔ Putting a tee-peg in the butt-end of your club helps to focus your mind on the correct wrist action in your backswing.

swingback until tee-peg points at ground

ensure good body turn at the top of backswing

2 Now rehearse your backswing. When your left hand reaches hip height, the tee-peg in the butt-end of the grip should be pointing at the ground just outside your right toe. This suggests a proper wrist hinge, which will set the club correctly in your swing. From there you can generate a steeper angle of attack into the ball.

There is no reason to fear shots from the rough; the proper wrist action will get you out of most trouble.

3 By pre-setting a steeper angle of attack in your backswing you can then strike down into impact, so maximize contact with the golf ball and minimize the amount of grass that gets trapped between club and ball. This is how you can generate good distance from the rough.

keep left wrist firm at impact

Inconsistency

Everyone misses greens. Even Tiger Woods, the best player in the world, only hits 75 per cent of the greens he looks at in an outstanding year. But if you find you're missing a lot of greens from the middle of the fairway, especially with no particular pattern and only a mid-iron in your hands, then that suggests a more serious problem is afflicting your game, one that needs immediate attention.

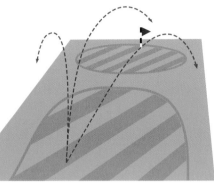

Inconsistent shots

CAUSE Faulty path or alignment?

aim or alignment could be at fault...

...or it could be the path of your swing

Inconsistency can be a result of any one of a number of factors. It may be a simple case of poor club selection; this will make you feel that you need to force your shots, which is bad news both for accuracy and for distance control. Worse still, even your well-struck shots will probably come up short of the green, and certainly short of the pin.

However, if you can honestly say that it's not a question of club selection, then it comes down to two things. If the ball-strike feels solid and you are still missing lots of greens, then it suggests a problem with your aim or your alignment. Let's face it, if you don't aim the gun correctly, you can't expect to hit the target. Failing that, it is likely that your swing path is to blame.

FIX

Check the fundamentals

You need to check your alignment, then your swing path. First, check your aim and alignment. Stand to the ball in what you think is good alignment, and then place your club along the line of your toes. Step back and see what this tells you. It could be that what you think is good alignment is in fact nothing of the sort.

To check to see if poor swing path is the culprit, analyze your divot mark after each shot; it should be pointing straight at the target. If it is pointing left of the target, that indicates an out-to-in swing path; if it points right of the target, you're swinging the club on an excessively in-to-out path. Either way, you'll know what corrective measures are necessary.

1

set-up to the ball as normal

2

place a club on your toes

3

check the alignment with your target

✔ The eye can sometimes play tricks. This drill confirms your alignment; no confusion.

CURE

Try "shaking hands" with the target

This is a great drill to help promote an on-line swing where it counts – through the hitting area. It requires a little imagination, but it should improve the accuracy of your mid-iron approach shots and get you hitting more greens. At first, you'll need to work on it at the range. But once you feel comfortable with it, you can use this form of visualization as a key swing-thought when you're on the golf course.

1 Start off by hitting a few "looseners", maybe with something like a 7-iron. This is just to get you into the swing of things and feel the ball coming out of the middle of the clubface. Now, time to focus. As you swing into impact and extend your right arm through the ball, imagine that you are reaching out to shake hands with the target.

2 Try it first in a practice swing. Freeze-frame the action when your right arm is horizontal to the ground through impact. Your right hand should be extended out towards the target, as if to shake hands with it. If that is the case, then you have achieved a good swing path through the hitting area. Try to replicate this in your actual swing, as you hit shots.

This "hand-shaking" swing-check gives you valuable feedback on the path of the club through impact, so you can identify potential faults.

shaking hands to the right of target suggests in-to-out swing path

if you shake hands to the left it indicates an out-to-in swing path

3 Those early practice swings enable you to see if your swing path through impact is crooked. If it is, your right arm will shake hands either to the left or to the right of the target. Shaking hands to the right of the target indicates an excessively in-to-out swing path, which will cause you to miss a lot of shots to the right, or possibly to hit a lot of hook shots.

4 Shaking hands to the left of the target suggests an out-to-in swing path, which means you pull a lot of iron shots and probably slice shots with the longer clubs in your bag. Repeat the correct "handshake" until you can get it right every time in your practice swing, then do it for real in your proper swing. It really works.

The centre of the green is your friend

In the last few holes of a major championship, 18-time major winner Jack Nicklaus revealed that he never aims at the flag, only at the middle of the green. He felt it was the smart play. It minimized his chances of missing the green and virtually guaranteed him a birdie putt – under pressure, that counts for a lot. So if Jack Nicklaus, arguably the greatest golfer who ever lived, ignores the flag, maybe we should all follow his lead?

The fact is, ignoring the pin and aiming all of your approach shots at the middle of the green is a very smart strategy; and I mean every single shot, whether it's a 9-iron or a 4-iron. This, in essence, builds in a bigger margin for error so that you have more green either side of the perfect golf shot. So if you stray slightly off line, as is often the case, you'll still find the putting surface.

Try doing this next time you play a competitive round. You'll be pleasantly surprised how many more birdie putts, rather than chips and bunker shots, you'll face.

Aim at the fattest part of the green, regardless of the pin position, as this offers the greatest margin for error.

aim for the
fattest part
of the green

Short irons

The shank

Let's not beat around the bush – well, not unless you're looking for your golf ball, anyway – the shank is the most demoralizing shot in golf. It happens when the ball is struck from the hosel of the club (the point where the clubhead meets the shaft), thus it can only be hit with an iron. This shot causes the ball to fly at an acute angle to the right of the target, often low and quickly, and usually heading towards the trees and bushes. It is a potential card-wrecker and a total morale-breaker, and it can unhinge even the sanest golfer. This one needs urgent attention.

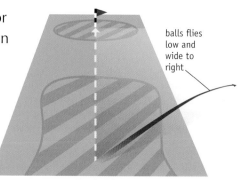

balls flies low and wide to right

Shanked ball

CAUSE Crossed paths

X Poor balance is often, although not always, at the root of a consistent tendency to shank iron shoots.

weight is back on heels at address

weight too far forward in downswing

1

2

If you hit a shank, you need to understand one very important thing about your golf swing; your clubhead is further away from your body at impact than it was at address. This is a matter of simple mechanics. At some point during your golf swing you have altered its path in such a way that instead of striking the ball out of the middle of the clubface, you've hit it out of the heel. The culprit? Well, it's more than likely that at some point in your downswing you are letting your weight fall forward on to your toes.

FIX

Posture and balance

Your instinctive reaction when you hit a shank may be to stand further away from the ball, but that only makes things worse. This forces you to reach for the ball even more, so you topple even further forward on to your toes. You need to work on establishing good posture and balance at address, with your weight firmly planted, and then try to maintain a constant spine angle in your swing. You may even need to feel as though your weight is more on your heels as you swing down, to correct the tendency to favour your toes. Also, try to feel that your hands are closer to your body as you swing down. Working on these measures together should help to rid you of the shanks.

maintain correct spine angle in backswing

2

work on good balance and posture at address

3

Feel your hands and arms closer to the body as you swing down and through.

1

CURE

The two-ball trick that works

This practice drill couldn't be simpler, and it's amazing what an effect it has on the shape of your swing. It's a great way to cure a case of the shanks. If you've got it bad, so to speak, then it may be wise to spend a whole session hitting shots in this fashion. Then you can move on to mixing it into your normal practice sessions, perhaps three drill-shots for every regular shot. The key is to try to get comfortable with this new movement as quickly a possible.

1 This drill is best rehearsed with a short iron; probably a 9-iron is best. Place three golf balls in a row, perpendicular to the target line, so that all the balls are touching. Then remove the middle golf ball. Now adopt your set-up, addressing the golf ball furthest away from you.

address the outer ball

aim to hit the inner ball

2 Now as you swing, ignore the golf ball you've addressed and attempt to hit the golf ball nearest you, leaving the other ball untouched. It sounds too simple to be of any benefit, but it's amazing what a difference it makes having that second ball in your field of vision.

3 You may initially hit both balls, which can be quite alarming, but persevere. This drill encourages a downswing motion whereby the club approaches impact from inside the line – not outside of it, as is the case with a shank or a slice. You won't shank the ball from that position. Instead you'll rediscover the middle of the clubface again.

✔ This drill quickly eradicates the swing-flaws that cause you to shank, and helps you to rediscover the middle of the clubface.

"Under pressure most people start tight at address and swing loose. When you're nervous, you've got to hold the club softly. Your grip pressure will instinctively become tighter as you hit the ball. It's like cracking a whip; soft to start and then tighter as you apply the hit."

Pete Thomson

THE SHANK

The pull shot

This shot has been discussed before – in the section on driving (*see p.24*) – but it is worth revisiting, since the "pull" is incredibly common with short irons. The shot-dynamics remain the same, with the golf ball starting left and continuing on that path. Even if the direction is not totally wild, it's likely to be a missed green, because a pull often travels further than a straight shot. That's because the clubface is square to the path of your swing, which produces a very solid hit. In this case, it's no cause for boasting: long and left is seldom a good place to be.

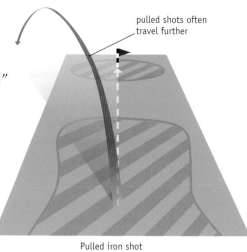

pulled shots often travel further

Pulled iron shot

THE PULL SHOT

CAUSE Where the shoulders go, the swing goes too

X Shoulders are "open" at address leading to an out-to-in swing path; this is a very common scenario.

shoulders aligned to left of target

1

2

The pull shot shares the same swing characteristics as a slice with the driver (*see p.14*); the path of the swing is across the line, from out to in. The main difference with a short iron is that the extra loft on the clubface creates lots of backspin, which negates the sidespin. The result is that the ball starts left and stays there; there is no curvature in the ball's trajectory mid-flight. With a short iron, the root cause can often be traced back to the set-up. If your shoulders are open and aligned to the left, then the swing tends to follow suit.

square shoulders
to target

match shoulder
alignment with
that of hips
and toes

FIX

Address those set-up issues

The first thing to look at is your set-up. It could be that the ball is too far forward; it's an easy habit to fall into with this type of shot. Position yourself so that the ball is further back in your stance, which is where it should be for a short-iron shot – right in-between both feet is ideal. This automatically brings your shoulders more into line; try it, you'll feel a difference immediately. Your swing will automatically come more into line too. As I have said before, the swing tends to follow the line of the shoulders.

As an extra measure, it also helps if you feel that your swing is more arm focused and less body-orientated. That will help to prevent your club from being thrown outside the line in your downswing, which of course is how the pull originates.

✔ Good alignment makes it is easier to swing your club on the correct path, leading to straighter golf shots.

make sure ball
is in centre of
your stance

THE PULL SHOT

CURE 1

Pivot over a flexed right knee

Once you have organized your
set-up and got into the habit of
aligning your shoulders correctly,
you'll find that your swing will
benefit and your tendency to pull
short-iron shots to the left will
diminish. There are still a couple of
useful swing-thoughts you might like to
focus on in your practice sessions. This one is
ideal for performing between shots. It trains an
effective body pivot, which will improve the
overall shape of your swing.

1 Start from a good
golfing posture and
hold a club at both ends,
with the shaft across the
back of your shoulders.

✔ Be aware of your alignment during your simulated swing, as your
shoulders turn and your knee flexes with your weight transfer.

turn to right
simulating
backswing

flex your
right knee
as you turn

keep knee
flexed as
you turn

turn to
left moving
weight to left

2 Turn your body to the right,
simulating a backswing and
shifting your weight on to your right
side. Keep your right knee flexed.
This creates resistance, increasing
the efficiency of your body coil.

3 Now turn to the left and
through, at the same time
transferring your weight on to your
left side. Repeat several times and
really try to get a sense your body
winding against the flexed right
knee, then unwinding powerfully
to the left side. Then hit shots,
maintaining the same core feelings.

CURE 2

Swing-path trainer

This is another effective drill, because it gets you focusing on the initial direction of your shots, which in turn can help to promote a more on-line swing path through impact. This is how to eliminate the pulled shot from your repertoire of undesirable golf shots.

1 Place a headcover on the ground in front of the golf ball, roughly ten paces away, and hit shots from the same spot. Your sole intention is to start the ball at the headcover, promoting that all-important inside angle of attack. It may take some doing, because you are having to overcome your well-ingrained tendency to do the opposite, However, once you have worked through this you'll notice that your shots do indeed start straight at the headcover.

2 Now, focus on a target in the distance and go for it. You should soon find that pulled iron shots are a thing of the past.

✔ Concentrating on your swing path to improve intial direction will ultimately help your consistency.

weight shifts from right to left foot in downswing

Think of three smart shots, not two risky ones

This is a course management idea to help you play better on long holes – especially monster par-5s, which can be very intimidating to the average golfer and thus are often the scene of ugly episodes and big numbers. So why is this advice to be found in the section on short-irons? It's simple: more often than not, on long holes such as here the end result of your endeavours is represented by a short-iron shot into the green.

As the heading suggests, the idea is based on the principle that three smart shots will on average produce lower scores than two risky shots. Too often on the tee of a par-5, golfers are pressured into hitting with a driver. They see the distance involved, focus on that, then go for the big hit, which often lands them in trouble. They're struggling to make par and the hole has only just begun! Disaster usually follows.

So, think about playing three smart shots. One of the secrets of playing long holes well is to break them down into three manageable parts – bite-sized chunks, if you like. It's a mental adjustment, more than anything else.

On a long and dangerous par-5 such as this, it's easy to get overly aggressive whilst attempting to punch the ball that bit further. It's a surefire path to a high score. However, if you hit two consecutive shots of 190m (210yds) – easily achieved with a hybrid or lofted wood – then you'll have no more than a short- or medium-iron into the green. That's an obvious birdie opportunity. And you haven't needed to take even the slightest risk. That's smart golf!

shot 2 from
the fairway

shot 3 to
the green

shot 1
from the tee

SMART GOLF

Wedges

The duffed chip

This is another high entry in the chart of embarrassing golf shots – potentially at the top of the list – although the term "hit" may be something of an exaggeration here. On a duffed-chip shot, the clubhead digs into the ground behind the ball and contact is often so poor that your ball hardly goes anywhere. There is also the danger of the double-hit, where the clubhead hits the golf ball again in the follow through.

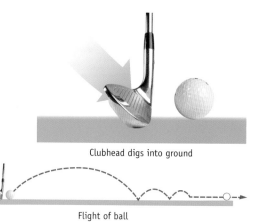

Clubhead digs into ground

Flight of ball

CAUSE Excessive hand and wrist action

✗ Too much hand and wrist action is the root cause of many chipping nightmares, as it makes consistent contact almost impossible.

hands behind ball

quick wrist hinge

scooping action

This problem tends to be most acute on clean lies, with closely mown grass or bare ground – it never seems to happen in rough. If that sounds familiar, you are probably employing way too much hand-and-wrist action in your swing. Excessive wrist action in the backswing is not the best of starts, as that sets the club on a very steep swing arc; immediately you've made it difficult for yourself to achieve a consistently solid strike. However, it's the more common scooping action with the right hand – in which the left wrist breaks down into impact and is overtaken by the right hand – that does most damage. This fault usually stems from a desire to want to help the ball into the air; however, your action does anything but.

✔ This is more of an arms-and-shoulders swing. The hands stay ahead of the clubhead at impact.

FIX

The only chip shot you'll ever need

The greenside chip is a straightforward stroke, and your technique should reflect that. This means eliminating any unnecessary hand and wrist action, and making more of a simple, compact, arms-and-shoulders swing. When trying to establish a good set-up, put the ball back in your stance, with your hands and weight forward. This will pre-set the correct impact factors, which is a big step in the right direction if you "duff" a lot of chip shots. Keep your weight forward and on the left side in your swing at all times and move the club back and forth with minimum wrist action. Your body should respond to the swinging motion with a small turn back and through. Keeping your left wrist firm, lead your club through the hitting zone with the back of your left hand.

✔ One of the secrets to good chip shots is to have your ball back in your stance, and your hands and weight forward.

THE DUFFED CHIP

105

start with a few long putts

CURE

Try to chip like you putt

For those who suffer from a chronic lack of confidence around the greens – or indeed for anyone who wants to develop a simple and reliable method – it's a good idea to think of the chip shot as simply a long putt with loft. The next time there's a golf tournament on television, watch carefully; you will notice that a lot of the leading pros employ this technique from close range. It's an extremely tidy little shot, one that produces consistent results. This is how it works.

press your hands forward

move the ball back in your stance

1 First, grab your putter and hit a few long putts across the green. For now, there's no need to worry about a target; this is just a process to get you thinking about your technique in isolation. Feel your hands and arms swinging back and forth in harmony with the turning motion of your body. There is, you will appreciate, no need for independent wrist action.

2 Now switch to a wedge. For this shot, position yourself so that the ball is closer to your right heel. Then angle the shaft of your club towards the target and place your hands in front of the golf ball. Some golfers also adopt their putting grip, but you may prefer to use your regular grip. You can also choke down on the grip. If you're very tall, you may prefer not to, but the benefit is that you effectively shorten the shaft, which gives you more control of the clubhead.

"From close range, think of the ideal chipping technique as pretty much like a putting stroke. You want the swing to be fairly short and compact, and you want it to have some rhythm. And, importantly, you don't want to take the club back any further than you must. Then you can accelerate through the ball and make solid contact."

Jim Furyk

3 Now make what feels like the same simple arms-and-shoulders swing as you did for your long putt. Try to feel as though you retain that "lean" in the shaft as you swing the club down into the back of the ball. Do not let the clubhead overtake the hands – that is disastrous – your hands must lead the clubhead, letting the loft toss the ball forwards on to the green.

4 The great thing about this technique is that you can apply it to almost any club, thus producing a range of shots with different height and spin characteristics. You don't have to change a thing: just let the loft on the club do the creative work for you.

 This technique is, with a bit of practice, easy to repeat. You'll soon develop a consistent strike with good judgement of distance.

Poor distance control

The wedges are the scoring clubs. Wedge play is where the tour pros do their best work, and where amateurs can save potentially handfuls of shots in a round of golf. Of course, one's aspirations are not always matched by reality. With shots in the 55–75m (60–80yds) range, it's distance control rather than direction that is the main problem. Too many wedge shots come up short of the flag or fall way too long. The problem is exacerbated in strong wind.

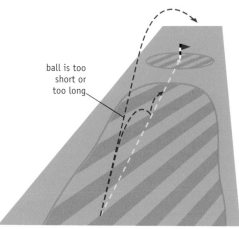

ball is too short or too long

Inconsistent length

CAUSE Lost control of your golf ball

X This swing is totally inappropriate for a wedge shot. There is no way you can control distance or direction.

If your distance is poor, you haven't got any control over your golf ball – and control is what these shots are all about. The problem usually occurs because your hand-and-arm action is out of sync with your body action; in essence, the two are fighting for supremacy in your swing. Sometimes your hands are too active, at other times the body becomes too dominant. Either way, it's impossible to develop any consistency in terms of clubhead speed and delivery through the impact area. That's why some shots fly further than others, often on wildly varying trajectories. It means lots of missed greens.

wrists fully hinged

take hands no further than shoulder height in backswing

FIX

Regain control of your golf swing

In order to be able to control the speed of your golf swing a little better, and thus exert more control over how far the golf ball flies through the air, you have to get the key elements of your swing working more in sync. Rather than making a full-out swing, which is where poor strikes and a lack of control stem from, try to make a "shoulder-to-shoulder" swing.

It helps if you make a couple of practice swings first. That will give you a feel for the correct movement, in readiness for the shot itself. The hands go to shoulder height in the backswing and shoulder height in the follow-through, controlled by the turning motion of your body and natural acceleration through the hitting area. There should be no abrupt hit at the ball, no violence! Just smooth acceleration through the ball.

✔ A three-quarter, shoulder-to-shoulder swing is easier to control, which will be reflected in the ball flight.

CURE

The clockface control system

Here is a drill to work on at the range. It will help you to develop a wedge system, so to speak, whereby you are able to see a yardage and then match the length of your swing to the distance you need to hit the ball. The more proficient you become at this, the more you will be able to hit your pitch shots with conviction. All you need for this drill is a bucket of balls and your wedge.

1 For the first ten shots, swing your hands back only as far as chest height. Imagine that you are standing in front of a giant clockface – your left arm should be in the 9 o'clock position. From there, swing through with natural acceleration. Make a note of the average distance you hit shots with this 9-o'clock swing.

2 For the next ten shots, swing your hands back a little further in the backswing, so that your left arm reaches ten o'clock. Maintain the same rate of smooth acceleration through the hitting area. As before, note the average distance you hit these shots. Discard the longest two shots and the shortest two, as they will not be representative.

Know your clubs

Apply this exercise to all three wedges in the bag to give yourself a total wedge system covering all the distances between, say, 45–90m (50–100yds). That's a real asset to your game.

✔ The sense of acceleration through the hitting area should remain constant. The length of your swing determines distance.

3 For the last ten shots, swing your left arm to 11 o'clock. Again, feel as you swing down and through with natural acceleration. Don't force things; this is a controlled golf swing. It has nothing to do with power.

4 You now have three different-length swings, and three different-length pitch shots. Write down the three sets of numbers on a small piece of paper and stick it to the underside of the shaft. When you refer to it on the golf course, you'll see that your 10 o'clock swing flies the ball, say, 70m (75yds) with that club. During a round of golf, such information will remove doubt, enabling you to execute shots with confidence.

POOR DISTANCE CONTROL

Loss of accuracy

The golf pros call anything around the 55–90m (60–100yd) mark the "scoring zone". They expect to get down in two shots from within that distance – and they frequently do. Indeed, short-game guru Dave Pelz once calculated that one of his students, former US Open champion Tom Kite, got up and down from within 55m (60yds) 85 per cent of the time over a three-year period on tour. That is an incredible statistic. On the other hand, far too many amateurs struggle with the accuracy of their pitching game. This is a shame, because in many respects – not least the fact that the clubshaft is short and power is not an issue – this is a relatively easy part of your game to put right. So let's get to it!

CAUSE Crooked swing path

✗ If you are too far inside, or outside, the ideal line coming down, you will never hit quality pitch shots.

club too far inside coming down

correct line swing plane

club too far outside coming down

swing plane

A lofted iron shot produces very little sidespin, so the direction in which the ball travels is very much determined by your swing path – in essence, the direction the clubhead is travelling when it meets the ball. So if you are finding that you miss a lot of greens, left and right with no real pattern, you have to find a way of getting your swing path into a more consistent groove whereby you can regain some of that lost accuracy. This will allow you to start setting your sights on the pin, rather than just hoping and praying that you'll land the ball somewhere on the green. It is a goal within everyone's reach.

take back club in slow motion

FIX

Focus on the path of your left arm

One simple way to achieve this is to actually forget about the golf club for a moment. Instead, watch your left arm travelling on the same line in the downswing as it did in the backswing. Go ahead and rehearse this in slow motion, maybe as a part of your pre-shot routine. Just watch your left arm as you move slowly through your backswing, then try to retrace that exact path as you swing down. Do it a few times, gradually building up to normal speed. You'll find that it definitely helps to improve your swing path, and you should see an improvement in your ball-flight and accuracy.

watch left arm

retrace path on downswing

✔ In this simple drill, focus on your left arm as you take it back and then down on the same path.

CURE

Four-steps to an effective on-line path

This drill helps to encourage a good swing path, which is obviously going to have a beneficial effect on the initial direction of your shots and, ultimately, the accuracy of your pitching. Try it in your next practice session, maybe one rehearsal drill for every three regular shots that you hit. You may find that it is quite a tricky manoeuvre to master, so it's wise to start off with practice swings. Once you start to feel comfortable with what you're doing, graduate to hitting shots.

be sure your aim and lignment is perfect

swing back until butt points at ground just behind ball

1 Take your pitching wedge and set-up to the golf ball. Be exact with your aim and alignment to be sure you get the most out of this particular drill. Poor alignment will drastically dilute the benefits.

2 Swing your club back into a position where your left arm is parallel to the ground and your wrists are fully set, with a 90-degree angle between your left arm and the shaft. Stop there. Look back and check the position of the shaft and the clubhead. The butt-end of the club should point at a spot on the ground in front of you, ideally one that is much closer to the golf ball than your toes. That represents a good swing plane. If you notice any significant deviation from this position, you should make the necessary adjustments to get your body into the correct "slot".

"To encourage the feeling of the hands, arms, and body moving together, make a three-quarter backswing and then pause momentarily. Then continue into your downswing and hit the shot. In that transition phase, make sure you keep the motion nice and smooth. If you rush it, you've blown it!"

David Leadbetter

✔ Pause to check that your club is in the correct position, then let your swing flow.

3 Without moving from this position, move your head back into its original position and focus on the golf ball. Try to complete your backswing with a full upper-body turn. You should find that your hands, arms, and club naturally adopt a comfortable position at the top of your swing.

4 From there, let the downswing flow in one continuous motion, just as you would with a regular shot. Make sure that your rhythm and tempo as smooth as you can, swinging through to a balanced finish.

Lack of "touch"

This problem doesn't necessarily arise from not striking the ball properly (although there's always room for improvement); it's more likely that you find judging distance troublesome. This is something that can afflict even the most accomplished players, and it tends to be most noticeable if you have not been playing a lot of golf, because your "touch" just isn't quite

there. Pros often describe it as being a bit "rusty". The symptoms are obvious. Even on straightforward chip shots the ball either races past the hole or pulls up way short. If there are any significant slopes on the green, the problem will be exacerbated. All too often you find yourself turning two shots into three – it's seldom the other way round.

CAUSE Unnatural acceleration

If your swing is too long, you have to decelerate into impact so that you don't hit the ball too far.

backswing too long

Constant and natural acceleration through the hitting area is at the heart of good distance control, because it improves the likelihood of a clean strike. And if you're striking the ball the same way every shot, you can predict more accurately how the ball will come off your clubface, how far it will fly through the air, and what it will do when it hits the ground.

The key to all this is the length of your backswing. If you are struggling to control the distance of your chip shots, you probably have the wrong length of backswing for any given shot. Too long, and you have to decelerate your club into impact in order to avoid hitting the ball too far; too short, and you have to hit the ball more aggressively to make up the distance.

make some practice swings to gauge length

FIX

Swing through more than you swung back

The most important thing to work on is your ability to make an appropriate-length backswing for every chip shot, as this allows you to accelerate the club smoothly through impact and send the ball the correct distance.

Get into the habit of making a couple of practice swings before each shot – practice swings that actually serve a purpose, not just a casual flick of the club back and through. As you do so, try to get a feel for the length of swing required to send the ball the correct distance. As a rule of thumb, make sure that the club travels further on the follow-through than it did on your backswing. This will instil in you the commitment to accelerate through impact, rather than quit on the shot.

✔ All good chip shots require natural, not forced, acceleration through the hitting area.

make appropriate length backswing

use natural acceleration

CURE

Chip to tee-pegs

If you are limited by the amount of practice time you have in a typical week, you should always favour the short game. Ask the tour pros and they'll say the same thing. This is the area of the game where you make or break your score. The practice drill shown here is simple and ideal for helping to restore your touch and feel for distance on chip shots. It gives you a greater appreciation of the relationship between height, spin, and roll – the key ingredients of any chip shot.

1 Grab a dozen or so balls and three clubs ranging from, say, an 8-iron to a lob-wedge. Park yourself on the edge of the green. Then walk on to the green and stick a tee-peg in the ground somewhere between you and the flag.

2 Now, starting with the least-lofted club hit three or four chip shots. Aim to pitch the ball next to the tee-peg. That's all. Just hit your mark and observe what the ball does once it lands.

3 Taking your next most-lofted club, repeat the exercise. Again, concentrate on making clean contact. Watch the ball's trajectory; in particular observe how it spins and rolls once it lands on the green.

4 Work your way up to the lob-wedge. As you continue with this drill, you are learning all the time about the characteristics of each shot. This is crucial information. It enables you to visualize a shot, match the right club to the job, and through the benefits of this practice drill execute it correctly, too.

5 Finally, a thought to take with you on to the golf course: always aim to land your golf ball as near to you as possible, and ideally on the flattest portion of the green. Chip shots are easier to judge on the ground than through the air, so it's good to get the ball running as early in its journey as possible. Also, flat spots will help to ensure a more predictable first bounce. If you're pitching the ball into slopes, it's much harder to anticipate how the ball will react.

LACK OF "TOUCH"

"Whether I'm 3 feet or 30 feet from the green, my aim is always to land the ball on the green as near to me as possible and let it roll like a putt."

Thomas Bjorn

Explore some less-lofted options

A lofted club is often the best choice around the greens. But there are occasions when it isn't strictly necessary and (whisper this quietly in the clubhouse) it might not even be the smartest play.

When the grass is closely mown and there are no obstacles between you and the flag, remember the old "Texas Wedge" – that is, a putt from off the green. The pros use this shot all the time, if the conditions are right, and so should you. It's relatively easy to judge and almost impossible to mess up. You may think you can chip it closer with a wedge (and maybe you can, once in a while), but if you average it out over ten balls, you'll find that you save more pars using your putter than you do with your wedge.

If the lie isn't perfect – maybe your ball is sitting in light rough – and again there are no hazards between you and the green, a chip with a lofted wood is another smart choice. Choke down on the grip, with the fingers of your right hand almost touching the shaft, and stand as close to the ball as you comfortably can. The swing itself is just a long putt hit with loft. It's controlled by your arms and a gentle rocking motion of your shoulders. There's no need to get fancy with your hands, since the clubhead will stay low, nudging the ball on its way.

A putt from the apron of the green is often the smart shot. Equally, from light rough a low-running chip shot with a lofted wood or hybrid might get the job done better than a wedge.

try a lofted wood
in light rough

try a putter
on closely
mown grass

Sand iron

No escape

There probably isn't another shot in golf that generates such doubt and apprehension, in some cases bordering on fear, as the greenside bunker shot. The sunny disposition of the typical amateur can become overcast at the mere sight of the "beached" golf ball. Why should sand create such extreme feelings? Well, this is a shot like no other – it's perhaps the only shot in golf that requires you to deliberately avoid striking the ball cleanly. This knowledge leads to one of the most common mistakes in bunkers, whereby the golfer will move huge quantities of sand at impact – so much so that all the energy in the swing is absorbed by the sand, and the ball fails to clear the front lip and comes back into the bunker.

Taking too much sand

CAUSE Right idea; wrong execution

✗ Some golfers tend to lunge at the ball, removing a lot of sand… but sadly not the golf ball.

1

2

Swinging your club on an out-to-in path on greenside bunker shots is technically correct. However, it is the way golfers go about this that causes problems. Some players lift the club on an exaggerated upward path, way outside the line; others will whip the club back on the inside as I have in this sequence. Either way, the tendency then is to apply the clubhead into the sand with a pronounced body-lunge, in an effort to get the clubhead swinging on that all-important out-to-in path. It's a disaster. There's no "zip" to the swing, the angle of attack is far too steep, and the clubhead removes a load of sand from the bunker – but sadly not the golf ball.

good blend of
arm swing and
body turn

1

2

✔ Set-up open to the target and then swing your club
along your aim lines.

3

4

FIX

Set-up correctly and swing freely

We need to tone down the changes you're trying to make in the swing. Okay, this is a bunker shot and you need to adapt your technique somewhat. But it is subtle changes, rather than drastic ones, that we're looking for here. Set yourself slightly open to the target line at address, with a slightly open clubface too. Once you've done that, you can swing along the line of your toes. You should avoid making an exaggerated outside-the-line backswing.

Adopt the same rules for your downswing. Swing the club down along your aim lines. The clubhead will indeed travel across the line, just as required. This, combined with the open clubface, ensures that the ball flies straight at the target.

NO ESCAPE

CURE

Make one-armed swings in the sand

This drill takes you through three stages of developing an improved bunker technique, ultimately resulting in you hitting better bunker shots than ever before. You'll find that you achieve this much more quickly than you'd imagine. You'll realize that there is no need to fear bunker play; indeed, you'll begin to understand why most tour pros prefer a bunker shot to an equivalent-length shot from rough grass. It is in many ways much easier to control.

✔ Make free swings with your right arm; get used to the clubhead splashing through the sand.

✔ Now put both hands on the club and make some practice swings, working on the same feelings.

1 Don't worry about a ball for now. Open the clubface and grip the club with your right hand only. Get into the habit of swinging the club freely, releasing it and splashing the clubhead through the sand. Listen to the sound of the broad flange thumping down into the sand. You'll start to appreciate the sensations of proper bunker play, and you'll quickly realize that it has nothing to do with brute force or throwing your body into the shot.

2 Next, move on to making swings with both hands on the club. Try to replicate the same sense of a free swing with your hands and arms, with the clubhead accelerating and releasing through the sand, not digging down too deep. Again, don't let your body dominate the action. This is one instance where you might be best served by letting your body move in response to the swinging motion of your arms, rather than the other way round.

3 Finally, put a ball in the sand and try to import the techniques you rehearsed in the drill into your actual swing. You should find that the club travels through the sand more easily on a shallower angle of attack. If you can achieve that consistently, the ball will come out every time. Then you can start working on your distance control, without any negative thoughts holding you back.

 If you can carry these feelings through into your actual swing, the ball will come out of the sand every time.

"The difference between a sand trap and a water hazard is the difference between a car crash and an airplane crash. You have a chance of recovering from a car crash!"

Bobby Jones

Thin or clean

This is the exact opposite of the "beached" ball problem on the previous pages. In this instance, the issue is too little sand, rather than too much. The clubhead barely takes any sand before impact, and the golf ball flies low and bullet-like, and thuds into the front lip. Whenever that happens there is a danger that the ball will come back at you, possibly even hitting you, which will incur penalty shots. It may also come to rest in your own footprint, creating a further challenge. Perhaps worst of all, if the front lip of the bunker is relatively low, the golf ball might clear it altogether but then travel two, three, or even four times the required distance, which could land you in even more serious trouble.

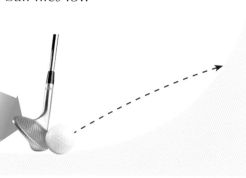

Not taking enough sand

CAUSE Angle of attack is too shallow

If you are not taking enough sand through impact, it's likely that you are addressing greenside bunker shots just like any other regular full shot from the fairway – in other words, with a square stance. If you stand too square in the sand, your angle of attack will be too shallow and the clubhead will not displace sufficient sand through impact. Without enough sand to cushion the blow, contact will be too clean. That's why the ball flies too low, and invariably too far.

If you are convinced that this is not the cause of the problem, ask yourself one important question. Are you trying to pick the ball off the sand too cleanly? That is a surprisingly common affliction, caused mainly by a misunderstanding of the correct bunker mechanics. If that rings bells with you, what you read over the next two pages should help you.

X If you stand too square at address, it is more difficult to generate the correct angle of attack in your swing.

open stance

club across the line at the top

FIX

Go back to basics

Remember, you must adopt a slightly open stance with the majority of greenside bunker shots. Align your feet and shoulders about 9–14m (10–15yds) to the left of the flag. Open your clubface, by which I mean aim it to the right of the target. The open stance will give your swing the out-to-in characteristic that creates the correct angle of attack – not too steep, but not too shallow either. The open clubface also ensures that the sand-wedge does its best work through impact, splashing down and through the sand, and propelling the golf ball up and over the front lip of the bunker.

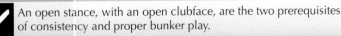

✔ An open stance, with an open clubface, are the two prerequisites of consistency and proper bunker play.

CURE

Focus on the sand, not the ball

This drill is something you need to rehearse first in the practice bunker, but it is also a great swing-thought to take on to the golf course with you. Indeed, some tour pros adopt this very principle in their own bunker play. If you've been having problems generating the correct impact factors – basically hitting the ball too cleanly or too heavy – then you'll find that the benefits of this drill will quickly filter through into your technique, and with quite remarkable consequences.

Without wishing to state the obvious, if you are catching the ball too cleanly, then you need to find a way to take more sand at impact. You must deliver the clubhead in a way that produces a "cushioned" blow.

1 Go to a regular bunker – nothing too severe. Now set-up to the golf ball as described on p.129, with your stance aligned to the left and the clubface open. As a general rule, it helps in bunker shots – as it does with most short shots – if you choke down on the grip slightly.

choke down on the grip

open the clubface

✔ Hover the club slightly behind the ball, and focus on that spot in the sand.

✔ As you swing, keep your eyes fixed not on the ball, but on your chosen spot in the sand.

2 Now, as you complete your set-up and get comfortable, concentrate not on the ball but on a spot in the sand behind the ball. That is the sole focus of your attention. Keep your eyes on that spot in the sand as you swing. That's your point of entry, so to speak.

3 Just splash the clubhead down on that spot and release your club freely through the sand. You don't have to worry about anything else. If your delivery is correct, and from the manner of your new improved set-up it should be, the cleverly designed sand-wedge will complete the job for you. Remember, what you're looking for is a nice shallow cut of sand from under the ball, not a shovel-load. The ball will come out every time.

Inconsistency

Getting out of the sand at the first attempt is one thing. Hitting the ball close enough to the pin to give yourself a makeable putt is another. This is something that many golfers, even those who play to a decent standard, struggle with. Your ball finishes on the green almost every time, but it feels as though its exact resting place is something of a lottery. Some shots finish short, others finish long. Every now and then you get one to come to rest roughly adjacent to the flag. There is no pattern, though, just general inconsistency.

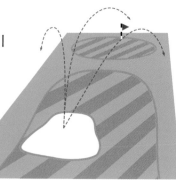

Inconsistent shots

CAUSE Cloudy mindset leads to vague execution

✗ A reasonable technique is one thing, but you still need to be able to judge distance – a problem for many golfers.

Gripping the club too tightly is often a cause of poor distance control, because a vice-like hold kills all "feeling" for the shot. So every golfer should start by relaxing their hold and gripping the club more softly.

More common, however, is a cloudy mind-set in terms of what exactly you are trying to achieve. This leads to little more than a "hit-and-hope" approach. There is no commitment to hit the ideal spot in the sand behind the ball and, perhaps more damaging, no concept of the appropriate length of swing and the acceleration required. The mechanics of a decent technique may be present, but the execution is poor.

FIX

Hit the same spot in the sand, and control distance with length of swing

Taking the same amount of sand for every shot, other than those where the ball has come to rest in an awkward lie, is a smart strategy. What constitutes the "correct" amount of sand is, in part, a personal thing. It also comes down to the type of sand in the bunkers on the course. If the sand is soft and powdery, it's better that you take more sand at impact than on a course where the sand is heavier and firmer. A bit of trial and error will help to establish your preference. Somewhere between 2–8cm (1–3ins) is typical.

What's important is that you endeavour to take the same amount of sand every time, and simply use the length of your swing to control the distance of each shot. Keep the rate of acceleration through the sand the same for every shot, increasing the length of your backswing to send the ball further.

work out how much sand you want to take...

...then do it on every shot

✔ Hit the same spot in the sand every time; control distance by varying the length of your swing.

INCONSISTENCY

CURE 1

Draw lines in the sand

It's easy to get yourself in a terrible mess with bunker play, especially if you are lacking confidence and fearful of this type of shot. This drill focuses on learning to hit the same spot in the sand by gaining a feel for the bottom of the swing arc. And, of course, once you learn to hit the same spot in the sand every time, you will find it much easier to judge how far the ball will fly. This is one of the secrets of becoming a better bunker player.

1 Draw a line in the sand. The easiest way to do this is to put a rake in the bunker and stand on it so it makes a clear imprint in the sand. Now adopt your address position.

 Practice with a line drawn in the sand; it's a great way to focus the mind on hitting the correct "entry point".

CURE 2

Open the clubface and then form your grip

This is a relatively elementary point, but it has merit. Many golfers make the mistake of forming their grip first and then twisting the clubface into an open position once they've settled over the ball. That's not good enough. The clubface more than likely returns to square at impact, which causes all manner of problems with distance control. This quick drill ensures that the clubface stays open throughout your swing.

1 Hold the sand-iron out in front of you and swivel the club loosely in your fingers, rotating the face clockwise until it is in an open position.

2 Your goal is to cut out a shallow divot of sand from the line using the back of the club to thump through the sand. Continue down the line. You'll experience some inconsistency initially, but you should develop a good feeling for what you are trying to achieve.

3 At the end of the line, place a ball slightly ahead of the line. Repeat the same swing that you've just rehearsed, thumping the clubhead into the sand on a shallow arc. Try to feel that you are just letting the ball get in the way. The ball will come out every time – a real boost to your confidence.

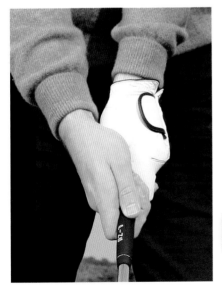

2 Now form your grip, making sure that the position of the clubface remains the same.

3 Do not re-grip the club as you move into your set-up position. Maintain the same hold, with the clubface open.

4 The clubface will now stay open throughout the golf swing – exactly what you need for good bunker shots.

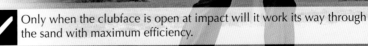

✔ Only when the clubface is open at impact will it work its way through the sand with maximum efficiency.

135

SAND-IRON

Sloping lies

By the very nature of a typical bunker's construction, sloping lies are inevitable at some point or other. Whereas on a closely mown fairway the golf ball will often roll off severe slopes and into a relatively flat spot, in bunkers the soft sand holds it in place, often perched in such a way as to force you to stand in the most awkward positions. From there, it is easy to make poor contact and fail to escape the sand or missjudge the ball's flight. The problem is most acute on upslopes and downslopes.

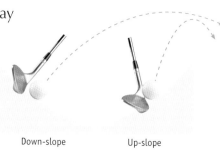

Down-slope   Up-slope

CAUSE Poor set-up leads to poor delivery

X If you lean into an up-slope, the angle of attack is often too steep so that you take way too much sand at impact.

It's an unlucky break when your ball finishes on a slope in a bunker, but the real problems stem from failing to adapt your set-up to the sloping lie. This immediately compromises your balance. You may not feel it much at address, but as soon as you start your swing you'll be thrown off-balance, making it impossible to control what the clubhead is doing. This means that you will almost always make poor contact, sometimes taking too much sand, sometimes not enough. Either way, the result is not good.

FIX

Match your body angles to the slope

The secret to success when you're playing a shot from a bunker slope is to adapt your set-up to suit the situation. This will aid your balance and promote the correct shape of swing to achieve good contact in the sand.

Up-slope: Put the ball forward in your stance and settle your weight back on your right foot; also "feel" that your right shoulder is significantly lower than your left, so that your shoulders are parallel to the slope. You can then swing in such a way that the clubhead naturally follows the contours of the sand. Your angle of attack becomes effectively normal. The ball will fly much higher than usual, though, and also stop very quickly on landing.

If you match your body angle to the slope, the angle of delivery will more than likely be correct.

1   2   3

The same rules apply on a down-slope: match your body angle to the slope to create the ideal angle of attack.

1   2   3

Down-slope: As before, get your shoulders as parallel to the slope as possible by putting most of your weight on your left foot. Feel that the right shoulder is a bit higher than usual. Once again, this enables you to swing the clubhead with the slope. However, you must pick the club up steeper in the backswing, with a quick wrist hinge to create the necessary steep angle of attack. Make an extra effort to stay down through the shot, keeping your clubhead low to the sand through impact.

SLOPING LIES

CURE

Trial and error is a great teacher

The great South African golfer Gary Player, a winner of nine major championships, would practice this drill for hours on end at the height of his playing career. And he was recognized – still is in fact – as the greatest bunker player ever. Recommendations don't come any stronger than that.

The concept could not be simpler. Find a bunker where you won't be disturbed and throw a handful of balls into the sand, in a variety of lies. Then go ahead and play each ball, making sure that you treat each shot with care and attention. Don't just go in there blasting away with gay abandon.

Try to use your imagination; experiment a bit. You'll learn more that way. On the next three pages are a few pointers (in addition to the advice on up-slopes and down-slopes on the previous pages) to help you tackle these different lies with conviction.

Plugged lie: A plugged lie, where the ball lands full-toss in the sand and half-buries itself in its own pitch mark, is the only greenside bunker shot where you should not open the clubface. Keep your clubface square and position the ball well back in your stance, closer to the back foot than the front. Your hands should be in front of the golf ball.

Pick your club up steeply in your backswing, with an early wrist hinge. Then thump the clubhead down into the sand. When a lie is as poor as this, that leading edge has got to "explode" the ball out. You can afford to be aggressive remember, there's plenty of sand to cushion the blow.

From a plugged lie you need to hit down harder, and more steeply, than with a regular greenside bunker shot.

Side-slopes: Golfers get in something of a tangle whenever the ball comes to rest on a side-slope in the sand – either with the ball above or below the level of the player's feet. But, once the necessary adjustments have been made to your set-up, they should not give you any major problems.

If the ball is above your feet, stand a little taller than normal and aim slightly to the right of the target to allow for a slight pull shot. Also choke down on the grip about 5cm (2ins). Then try to swing the club around your body, on what feels like a flatter swing plane.

stand taller

keep your spine angle constant

✔ It's easy to catch this shot heavy, so be aggressive and really accelerate the club through the sand.

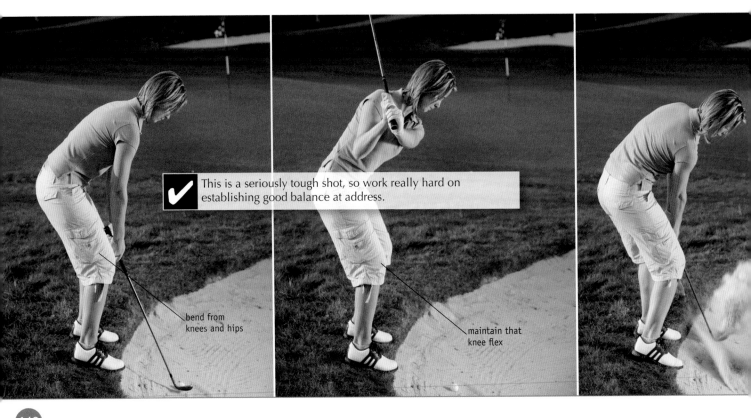

✔ This is a seriously tough shot, so work really hard on establishing good balance at address.

bend from knees and hips

maintain that knee flex

get body out of way

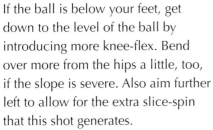

If the ball is below your feet, get down to the level of the ball by introducing more knee-flex. Bend over more from the hips a little, too, if the slope is severe. Also aim further left to allow for the extra slice-spin that this shot generates.

In contrast to the previous shot, this situation requires a steep up-and-down swing plane, so make your swing a little more hands-and-arms orientated, with not so much movement from the body. Just stab the clubhead down into the sand behind the ball.

 This shot is often best tackled by playing a splash shot with a less-lofted club than a sand-iron.

Mid-range splash: This is one of the toughest shots in golf; even the pros don't relish this one. It's neither a full bunker shot, nor a short one; it's somewhere between the two – say, around the 27–37m (30–40yds) mark. So take a leaf out of the pro's book. They'll often leave the sand-iron in the bag – far too much loft to comfortably generate that much distance from sand. Instead, they go with a pitching-wedge or even a 9-iron. Open your clubface slightly and play a conventional splash shot, only with less loft. Experiment in the practice bunker before you try it in a proper round of golf. Then you can get used to controlling ball-flight and distance.

141

Sand can train the perfect strike

Understandably you may feel that there is no upside to being in a bunker. It does, after all, suggest that you've just hit a wayward approach shot. But the bunker can be a good place to be in your practice sessions, and not just to work on your greenside shots. It is actually one of the best locations to improve your ball-striking on full shots.

Take any club from a 9-iron to a 6-iron. Then find a bunker with a flat area of sand from which you can hit shots. The first thing you'll notice is that sand offers a less secure footing than the fairway, which is one of the reasons this is such a great drill. You can't lunge at the ball, because you'll simply lose your footing. The shifting sand forces you to make a smooth, unhurried transition from the top of backswing into your downswing. All good players share that quality. As you hit shots, think "tempo and balance".

This practice drill also gives you great feedback on the quality, or otherwise, of your ball-striking. Sand accentuates the effects of a poor strike, so if you hit the shot even a little bit heavy you'll find the ball travels nowhere near what you'd expect for that particular club. This will focus your attention on hitting the ball cleanly, with a slightly descending blow. If you can improve your ball-striking in sand, it will translate into perfect ball-turf contact in the fairway. That's how the pros generate so much backspin on their iron shots, so that the ball spins back when it lands on the green.

Oh, one final thing. Rake the bunker when you've finished. You don't want to get on the wrong side of the greens keeper or, indeed, the members at the club!

Vijay Singh practises this drill all the time; it is one of the best ways to discipline yourself to strike the ball with a slightly descending blow.

Putter

Ball misses left

How well you putt the ball along the ground bears almost no relation to how well you can hit it through the air. That is why putting is often described as the game within a game. There are many ways to make a putt – and, regrettably, many more ways to miss one. The pull, where the ball misses the hole consistently to the left, is extremely common. It occurs – or at the very least is most evident – on short putts from anywhere inside 2m (6ft). It's an invidious business, and many players find that its negative impact spreads throughout the rest of their game.

ball misses left

CAUSE Breaking down at impact

1 address looks fine

2 left wrist is weak in backswing...

3 ... so ball misses to the left

✗ If you allow the left wrist to break down as you swing the putter through impact, you will almost certainly miss the putt left.

If many of your putts are missing left, then the most likely cause is that your left wrist is breaking down, or collapsing, at the moment when the putter is delivered to the back of the ball. In effect, the putter-face effectively overtakes the hands, closing the putter-face and pulling the ball to the left. You are probably unaware of what is happening to your wrist, because habit will have made it feel comfortable.

FIX

Left wrist stays firm through impact

As with a lot of golfing faults, the first thing you need to focus on is the quality of your set-up. Analyze the key components of how you stand to the ball and see if the problem isn't in there somewhere. Your left wrist position is especially important, so begin by setting it at a good angle at address. Your hands should be over, or very slightly in front of, the ball. This isn't a rule set in stone, but if you are missing a lot of putts to the left it is advice worth heeding.

Then try to make sure that your left wrist doesn't break down or, as I described opposite, collapse through impact. As you swing the putter into the back of the ball, make sure that the back of your left hand and wrist continue to look down the target line.

keep left wrist firm

keep putter-face square

3

✔ Set your left wrist at a good angle, then maintain that as you complete your address position.

BALL MISSES LEFT

147

CURE 1

Brace yourself

If you've grown comfortable putting in a certain way, even if it is the wrong way, then a habit has been formed. Consequently, making changes to your putting stroke can be quite difficult. That's why drills such as this one are so effective, because they use a simple prop to help kick-start the change. This putting drill in particular accentuates the correct feeling in your stroke, which then enables you to integrate it more easily into your actual technique. What's important here is that you wear your watch!

adopt a light grip pressure

1 Place a pen, a pencil, or even a ruler underneath your watchstrap on the back of your left wrist. It should feel almost like a splint on your wrist, and it effectively "locks" the wrist into a relatively straight position.

2 Set-up to the ball as described on the previous page, and be especially mindful of the angle in your left wrist at address, as you'll need to maintain this when you swing the putter through the ball.

This drill quickly instills in you the feeling of keeping the left wrist firm as you deliver the putter to the ball.

hands and wrists stay passive in backswing

pen prevents left wrist breaking down at impact

3 Now make a backswing, trying to minimize excessive hand-and-wrist action. Again, the "splint" is an effective training aid, as it holds your left wrist in place and stops you getting too "handsy".

4 You'll find that your left wrist stays firm, the putter is less inclined to overtake your hands through the hitting area, and, crucially, the putter-face stays square. After a few tries, remove the splint from under your watch strap and work on the same feelings.

CURE 2

A cack-handed approach

Let's focus on that left wrist position again, because that's a major problem. One possible solution is to switch your hands on the grip, so that your left hand is below your right. This is often referred to as a cross-handed, or "cack-handed", grip. The reason I mention it here is that it can completely eradicate the tendency to let your left wrist break down at impact.

move left hand below right

keep putter low to the ground

keep wrists firm

1 Stand to the ball in your usual putting fashion with a conventional grip, and then simply switch hands so that your left hand is below your right. There are no hard-and-fast rules on exactly how you position your hands, but it is not a bad idea to have your palms facing, with your thumbs pointing down the centre of the putter-shaft. That is then a neutral hold.

2 Now make some practice putting strokes. You'll notice straight away that your left wrist automatically holds its position throughout the stroke. It stays firm. You will no longer tend to let the angle in the back of your wrist break down.

3 Keep working on this technique. It's not for everyone, but many golfers find that once they've tried this approach to putting, they never go back. Indeed, some of the world's top players adopt this grip.

match angle of back of left hand to angle of putter-face

✔ Putting with your left hand below the right has the advantage that your left wrist tends to hold its position through impact.

"I like my arms to feel long at address, almost fully extended and very soft. This encourages a free-swinging motion back and through, and I believe long arms enhance feel and promote a stroke that is easy to repeat."

Phil Mickelson

BALL MISSES LEFT

151

Ball misses right

If your misses tend to favour the right-hand side of the hole, then you are pushing your putts – again you'll notice this most acutely from anywhere inside 2–2.5m (6–8ft). This is perhaps a little less common than pulling putts to the left, but the end result is the same. Instead of picking your ball out of the hole and walking to the next tee, you're staring at another putt. As you may well know, if that happens too often it gets extremely tiresome.

ball misses right

CAUSE Poor path, poor aim ... or both

✗ An excessively in-to-out stroke will cause you to miss a lot of putts to the right.

putter too far inside target line going back

target line

pull is pushed to the right

1

2

The difference between success and failure in golf can be measured in mere fractions. The putt may be the shortest of strokes, but that doesn't make it any easier. If your putts are missing to the right of the hole, either the putter-face is fractionally open at impact or your stroke path is slightly in-to-out. It may be the subtlest of errors but, as I said, golf is game of fractions – and putting is a game of fractions within fractions!

step back to check the aim of your putter-face

run putter along a flag stick to train an on-line stoke

FIX

Take dead aim and fix the path

The two issues you need to look at are the aim of the putter and the path of the stroke. First, check the alignment of the putter-face. You can ask a friend to watch you or, failing that, try this simple routine. Stand to the ball and aim your putter at the hole; something in the region of a 1.5m (5ft) putt is ideal. Then, without altering the position of the putter-head, crouch down behind the line so that you can see where the putter is aiming. You may find that what you think you saw from above actually looks quite different from behind the line. Right then and there you may have identified the likely cause of your problem.

To check the path of your stroke, place the flag stick on the ground with one end resting next to the centre of the cup. Now adopt your address position with your putter resting on top of the flag stick. Then rehearse your stroke. On a short putt like this, the putter should go straight back and through. Any flaws will be obvious because the putter will deviate from the flag stick at some point during the stroke.

✔ If you can train a more on-line stroke you'll hole more putts, it's as simple as that.

CURE 1

Brush it in

Britain's greatest ever golfer, six-time major winner Nick Faldo, is a great advocate of this practice drill. Indeed, he rehearsed it in the build-up to one of his greatest tournament victories, the 1992 Open Championship at Muirfield. The aim is to train a stroke whereby the putter-face travels through towards the hole on the correct path and with good face-alignment, qualities that are sadly lacking if you miss a lot of short putts.

3 You then need to introduce that feeling and technique of swinging the putter through square and on the correct path into your actual stroke.

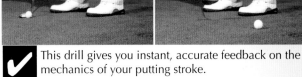

✔ This drill gives you instant, accurate feedback on the mechanics of your putting stroke.

1 Start by finding a straight putt of 90–100cm (3–4ft). Address the ball as you would normally.

2 Without making a backswing, brush the ball towards the hole. Keep your left wrist firm, with the back of your left hand and the putter-face looking at the hole as the ball is sent on its way. If you can get the ball rolling straight into the centre of the hole, the putter-face is square and the path is good.

CURE 2
Listen for the ball dropping into the hole

Another possible reason for missing more than your share of short putts to the right is looking up too soon, which interrupts the flow of the putter just as it's about to strike the golf ball. This tried-and-tested drill helps to cure that tendency. You should rehearse it first on the practice putting green; once you are accustomed to it you can take it on to the golf course.

1 Address a short putt, one that's in the region of 1.5–2m (5–6ft).

2 Keep your head rock-steady throughout the stroke, and do not look up until you hear the sound of the ball dropping into the hole (or not, as the case may be).

3 The long-term effects should be positive, as this commitment to keeping your head still reduces the tendency to make a poor stroke. Try it and see.

✔ Keeping your head down until the ball drops into the cup prevents you from disrupting the flow of your stroke.

BALL MISSES RIGHT

Lip-outs

These occur when the golf ball catches the rim of the hole and spins out, and they're a fact of life on the greens. But if you find that it happens to you rather more than, say, any of your usual playing companions, then that suggests something more than plain bad luck. It indicates a pattern to your putting that positively encourages lip-outs – and that is not good, to say the least. This trend requires your attention.

Ball spins out of hole

CAUSE Too aggressive

This situation has probably arisen because you are hitting your short putts too aggressively, trying to force the ball into the back of the hole. Consequently, anything other than dead-centre causes the ball to spin out. The majority of tour pros strike their short putts very firmly into the back of the hole, but attempting to emulate that approach is fraught with problems. For one thing, your typical professional spends many hours a week holing short putts, and that brings with it a certain amount of confidence, not to mention the necessary skills to execute it confidently on the golf course. Also, the putting surfaces in a pro tournament are better than those most amateurs play on. The holes are also cut every day and therefore have less "traffic" around them, which means that there are fewer imperfections to knock the ball from its path.

overly aggressive stroke

 Put simply, if you hit the ball too hard it has more of a tendency to lip-out.

FIX

Train a more evenly-paced stroke

The best advice is to try to develop a smoother, more evenly-paced putting stroke. Think in terms of stroking the ball gently into the hole from short range, rather than "banging" the ball into the back of the hole. Stand over the ball and make a point of gripping the club softly; then exhale slowly just before you are about to start your stroke. This releases the tension in your hands and body and promotes a smoother stroke, with less of an abrupt hit at the ball. It should help the timing of your strike considerably.

keep a neutral but firm grip on putter

accelerate smoothly through impact

CURE

Clap your hands, and then putt

There is little doubt that a great number of club golfers putt poorly – or at least inconsistently – because they allow far too much independent or excessive movement in the stroke. This upsets the path of the putter, causing a crooked stroke. The practice drill below gets right to the heart of that problem, reducing the putting stroke right down to its barest, purest form. It helps to train a putting stroke where everything works together as a cohesive unit. Thus, there is less likelihood of upsetting the pure flow of the putter straight back and through.

✔ Swing your hands and arms, while keeping wrist action to an absolute minimum

1 Adopt your normal address position, only without the putter in your hands. Then bring your hands together, palms facing, as if you are about to clap. Try to make sure that your shoulders and toes are parallel with the ball-to-target line. This in itself will promote a consistent path in your stroke.

2 Now swing your hands and arms back and forth, nice and smooth, basically simulating a putting stroke. Concentrate on keeping your hips and legs very steady, as if set in stone, and your head equally still. To help with this, you might want to focus on a spot on the green where the ball would ordinarily be.

3 The next stage is to replicate all this in your actual putting stroke. Repeat the same routine, bringing your hands together, palms facing one another, as you place them on the grip. Ideally, both thumbs should point down the centre of the shaft. This ensures that your hands are working together in the stroke rather than fighting one another, which is what tends to happen if you place your hands awkwardly on the grip.

✔ Now as you putt, feel your hands and arms working in the same way as with the previous drill.

4 Try to feel that the stroke is controlled by a gentle rocking motion of your shoulders, the arms swinging the putter back and forth with very little independent hand-and-wrist action. It is worth stressing again that your hips and legs should remain steady and your head still.

5 Only look up when the ball is on its way. Repeat several times. You'll find that you soon develop a more consistent and evenly paced putting action, due to the fact that there are fewer moving parts in the stroke. The strike will become more consistent and the initial line of your putts should soon improve.

LIP-OUTS

Not enough speed

If you are finding that the golf ball frequently pulls up short of the hole, the chances are it occurs more on mid- and long-distance putts than from close-range. Constantly leaving the ball short is a particularly wearing experience.

It's also costly to your score, because your putts don't actually threaten the hole – you never even give yourself a chance. There is, after all, no recorded evidence or likelihood of a hole coming to meet the ball!

CAUSE Deceleration into the ball

backswing is too long...

✗ If your backswing is too long there is no way you can consistently judge the weight of your putts.

... causing deceleration into impact

1

2

This is almost certainly caused by the acceleration, or rather the lack of it, in your putting stroke. Ironically, it often comes about as a result of a stroke that is not too short, as you might expect, but in fact too long. The overly long backswing forces you to decelerate into impact to avoid sending the ball racing away across the green past the hole. And 99 times out of 100 that deceleration leaves the ball way *short* of the hole. It's actually very difficult to decelerate and still hit a putt the appropriate distance. It just hardly ever happens.

FIX

Promote a sense of natural acceleration

There are many very contrasting putting techniques that all work, but there are certain characteristics shared by all good putters. An ability to judge the running speed of the ball across the green, so that your putts either go in or come to rest merely "tap-in" distance from the hole, is one such characteristic.

It is often referred to simply as "good feel" and it stems from an ability to maintain a constant and natural acceleration through the ball, controlling the distance of each putt with the length of the backswing. That is your key to judging distance. The sense of acceleration should feel the same whatever the length of the putt; you just make a progressively longer swing the further you are away from the hole.

✔ The key for any putt is to produce a length of stroke that allows smooth and natural acceleration through the ball.

NOT ENOUGH SPEED

CURE 1

Train the correct length stroke

This drill really couldn't be simpler, but it is amazing the effect it has, especially if you have been afflicted by your putts regularly falling short of the hole. It will help you to appreciate the feeling of making a smoothly accelerating stroke and, as a result, get more of your putts up to the hole-side.

second tee-peg   first tee-peg   third tee-peg

1 Place a tee-peg in the ground and a ball next to it. Then place a second tee-peg in the ground, say, 15cm (6in) behind the first one. Then place a third tee-peg in the ground double that distance in front of the middle tee-peg. Now address that ball.

address with ball at first tee-peg

swing putter back to second tee-peg

swing through to third tee-peg

2 Hit the putt, swinging the putter-head as far back as the second tee-peg and through at least as far as the third tee-peg. Thus, the follow-through is twice as long as the backswing, which encourages a smoothly accelerating stroke through the impact area.

3 Now apply this method to a variety of different-length putts, which requires different-length strokes. The principle always remains the same: always make your follow-through at least twice as long as your backswing – this is the way forward.

CURE 2

Watch the gap

I touched on the problem of unnecessary head movements earlier in the chapter (*see p.158*), but it is worth revisiting. The fact is, hitting weak putts that pull up short of the hole can be a consequence of looking up too early, of peeking to see whether or not the ball is going in the hole. If we get down to the nitty-gritty, it is often down to anxiety and a lack of confidence.

1 Address a putt as normal, only this time leave a small gap between the putter-head and the golf ball.

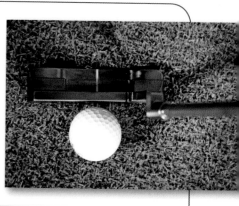

focus on gap between putter and ball

stay focused on same spot throughout stroke

2 Focus on the gap, not on the ball, as you putt. This helps to keep your head steady, and in the same position it was in at address. And that's good news for the putting stroke. It means that the path of the putter won't be upset by any swaying of the head and upper body. You'll strike your putts more sweetly, and on a more consistent basis.

NOT ENOUGH SPEED

Too much speed

Giving your putts too much speed, so that ball often races past the hole, has little merit – save, perhaps, for the fact that you'll be getting a clue as to the line of your next putt from the other side of the hole. But this is clutching at straws. And don't take any comfort from those who might utter the inane words "never up, never in". It doesn't really do anyone any favours to put a gloss on a putt hit too hard, because it's still a poor putt.

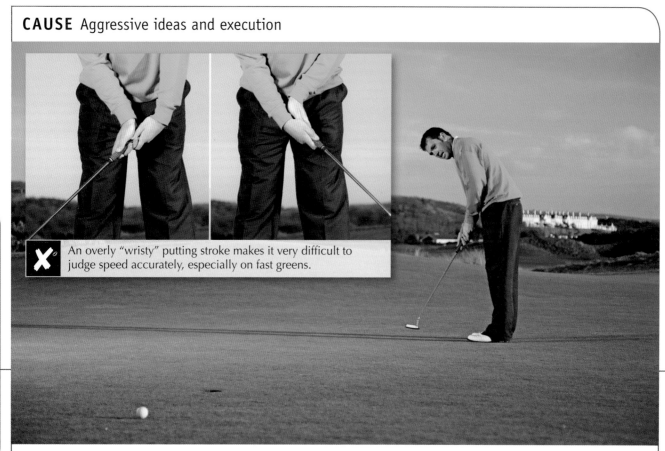

CAUSE Aggressive ideas and execution

An overly "wristy" putting stroke makes it very difficult to judge speed accurately, especially on fast greens.

The reason the term "never up, never in" is so unhelpful is that it implies you at least gave the putt a chance. You gave it nothing of the sort. If a putt is hit so hard that the ball races 2m (6ft) or so past the hole, then nothing was going to stop it – certainly not the hole, which it would have rolled straight over. Putts that are hit too hard are frequently the result of a misguided attempt to give the putt "a chance".

Alternatively, a pattern of aggressively judged putts can indicate a more serious problem with your stroke, and this nearly always takes the form of some kind of independent hand-and-wrist action or a basic lack of synchronization between the arms and body. The result is an erratic rate of acceleration through the ball, leading to a pattern of inconsistency that may indeed favour too much speed.

FIX

Speed and synchronization

First of all, understand what constitutes the correct pace for a putt. On that topic, as indeed with all things related to the short game, there is no greater authority than Dave Pelz. His scientific tests concluded that the optimum pace for a putt is such that the ball would, if it weren't stopped by the hole, finish 46cm (18in) past the hole. That is the pace that gives you the best chance of making a putt. And if it doesn't go in, you're merely left with a tap-in return putt. No drama there.

The excessive independent hand-and-wrist action might take longer to fix. You need to get to a position whereby you start to feel that a rocking motion of your shoulders creates the momentum of the stroke, and that your hands and arms then swing the putter in harmony with that motion. Everything should work together. The two drills over the page will further assist you in that ambition.

✔ Hands, arms, and shoulders need to be working together throughout the stroke.

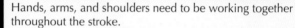

✔ Once you start to consistently judge the correct pace of your putts, the ball will find the hole much more frequently.

CURE 1

Rock the shaft to feel a connected stroke

The objective in this drill is to eliminate independent movement and get the body, the hands, the arms, and the putter all moving together as a team. Everything stays "connected" in your stroke.

✔ With a second club held between your chest and arms, rock the shaft up and down and let your hands and arms respond to that motion.

1 Trap a golf club under your armpits, so that the shaft runs across your chest. You could also use a rolled-up umbrella.

2 Adopt your putting stance and use the motion of your body to rock the shaft up and down as the hands and arms swing the putter back and forth. The club should remain firmly in place. Keep your head still throughout.

3 You should begin to appreciate the feeling of the whole upper body and your arms working as a cohesive unit. Remove the shaft from under your arms, and try to replicate the sensation in your actual stroke. Then you're right on track.

CURE 2

Staggered putting drill trains good feel for distance

This drill helps you to develop the all important "good feel" that I referred to earlier in the chapter (*see p.161*). This will have obvious benefits, in that you won't hit quite so many putts way past the hole. Your ability to judge speed will improve no end.

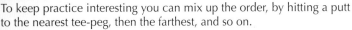

✔ To keep practice interesting you can mix up the order, by hitting a putt to the nearest tee-peg, then the farthest, and so on.

1 Place a row of tee-pegs in the ground, starting at about 3m (10ft) away and thereafter at intervals of about 1m (3ft). Continue for as long as space permits, up to a maximum of about 15m (50ft).

2 Hit the first ball to the first tee-peg, then the second ball to the second tee-peg, and so on. Every putt you hit improves your feel for distance. Using one ball at a time closely replicates an on-course situation, where you have only one chance at each putt. An hour or so a week at this drill will pay major dividends. It trains you to relate what you see to what you feel in your putting stroke – a valuable skill when it comes to judging distance.

TOO MUCH SPEED

167

Miss on the "low side"

Judging breaking putts is a very exacting discipline, because even the slightest slopes on the green tend to exaggerate your shortcomings in the putting department. The common consequence is missing on the so-called "low side", where the golf ball takes more borrow than was either anticipated or allowed for. It's a miserable outcome, because even before the ball has completed half its journey to the hole it is clear that it has no chance of finding its target. Indeed, once a ball is running on the low side, even if the pace is relatively good it can still get swept quite some distance beyond the hole.

Ball misses on the low-side

CAUSE Misread or mishit? You decide.

1

2

There are two possible factors at work when you miss a putt on the low side. You either misread the putt and therefore didn't allow for enough break in the first place (an extremely common scenario with most amateurs). Alternatively, your stroke didn't send the ball in the direction you initially intended. Identifying which of these two factors is most relevant to your stroke is the key to instigating the appropriate fix.

ball misses on the low side

 On a right-to-left putt such as this, it's all too easy to miss on the low side.

FIX

Putt to a "breaking point"

I will deal with misreading a putt over the page. First concentrate on helping to start the ball on the correct initial line so that it can then take the break and have a good chance of dropping into the hole. It comes down to putting to a "breaking point" – a method used by many tour pros.

Identify how much of a break there is on a putt, say, 1m (3ft) to the right of the hole. Then visualize an imaginary target on that exact spot – maybe an old pitch mark or a discoloration on the green. This spot, or "break", should be the focus of your attention. Forget the hole; just hit a straight putt at your imaginary target. Without making any adjustments, you're far more likely to strike the putt sweetly. Then you simply let the slope of the green take care of the rest.

look for breaking points on green

1

hit a straight putt and let the break take care of the rest

break

2

169

CURE 1

Practise putting to an imaginary target

On sloping putts many golfers aim too straight and try to steer the ball on to the right line by changing their stroke – a fundamental mistake. This first drill takes you beyond the idea of putting to a "breaking point" and aims to help you get into the habit of setting the ball off on the correct line and at the correct speed. That, along with a talent for reading the greens, is the key to success on sloping putts.

1 On your home course, locate a putt for which you are familiar with the break. Around 7–9m (25–30ft) is ideal for the purposes of this exercise. Place a tee-peg to one side of the hole, equivalent to the amount of break on that putt. Let's assume it is 50cm (20ins) to the right of the hole.

CURE 2

Take more care when you read putts

There is an art to reading putts, but it is a technique that can be learned. You just need to know where to look. Here are a few ideas to accelerate the learning process.

As you walk from the fairway towards the green, look for the highest point around the green; the land will tend to fall from that direction.

Watch the other golfers in your group and see how their chips and putts react as they approach the hole; you can learn a lot from your playing partners, and even from your opponent … but keep your eye on the ball!

✔ The tee-peg is now your target. Forget about the hole – it is of no consequence for the purpose of this drill.

2 Set-up to the ball as if you are putting to the tee-peg, then set the ball off on that line at what you think is a perfect pace. It's just like hitting a straight putt. Let the slope on the green do the work.

3 On the golf course, you can't place a tee-peg in the green and use that as your target, so use your imagination. The principle is the same: identify the break on the putt, visualize an imaginary target to the side of the hole, forget the hole itself, and hit a straight putt at your imaginary target.

If you read putts from behind the ball, as you should, stand the same distance from the ball every time, on every putt. Your eyes will then get used to a certain perspective.

A putt is most susceptible to break at the end of its journey, when the ball is travelling at its slowest speed, so pay particular attention to the slopes around the hole.

If you miss a putt, never turn away in disgust. Watch closely as the ball travels past the hole; that will tell you much about the line of the return putt you're about to face.

It's all a state of mind

The mechanics of the putting stroke are clearly important – without a good technique a golfer will always struggle to putt consistently well. Chance might suggest that any golfer can hole putts from time to time. But in reality you need a good technique in order to strike the ball properly and set it off on the correct line and at the correct pace. That has nothing to do with chance, and everything to do with technical prowess, which is why we have dedicated such a comparatively large proportion of this book to the art of putting. It is, however, important to differentiate between what you do on the practice putting green and what you do on the golf course during a competitive round. Save the major technical work primarily for your practice sessions. On the golf course, you need to immerse yourself in a very different mind-set.

Try to develop a pre-shot routine for putting. Initially, you will need to work on this, but repeat it often enough and it will become part of your subconscious thought process. Use that routine to treat every putt the same, whether it's on the 3rd green for a birdie or on the 18th green for a crucial par. At the end of the day, they all count as just one stroke. It's invaluable if you can train yourself to treat them this way; go through your routine and take the same amount of time on every putt. Don't suddenly become more careful just because you perceive it to be an important putt. That just places more pressure on you. Stick to your routine. You've got a job to do on every putt. Just do it!

Good putting is a balance between sound technique and good feel for distance. The further you are away from the hole, the more you need to think about "feel" and the less you need to think about technique. From anywhere beyond 12m (40ft) you need to be thinking mostly about rolling the ball at the perfect pace for that putt. You may find it helps to visualize an imaginary 1m (3ft) circle around the hole, then just focus on rolling the ball into that circle. If you hit your putts with good pace, you'll hole your share. The worst scenario is that you'll have a tap-in for your next putt.

target zone

Glossary

Address position
A golfer's set-up to the ball.

Approach shot
A shot played into the green.

Apron
The closely mown area of grass between the putting surface and the surrounding fairway or rough.

Bare lie
A golf ball sitting on a patch of ground with little or no grass.

Bounce
The wide flange on the sole of a sand-iron.

Break or Borrow
The degree by which a ball is affected by slopes on the green.

Choke
When a golfer loses his nerve and collapses under pressure.

Choke down
The process of holding the club further down the grip.

Divot
The turf dislodged, not always, at the moment of impact.

Divot mark
The hole in the ground that results from a divot being taken.

Draw
A shot that moves, subtly, on a right-to-left trajectory through the air.

Effective clubhead speed
The successful application of the clubhead to the golf ball, where the angle of attack, path, and clubface angle are all correct and appropriate for that shot.

Fade
A shot that moves, subtly, on a left-to-right trajectory through the air.

Grip
Either your hold on the club or the rubber handle that you hold.

Heavy
The clubhead makes contact with the ground before it strikes the ball, as in "hitting a shot heavy"; also known as "fat contact" or simply a "duff".

Hook
A shot that moves, severely, on a right-to-left trajectory through the air.

Hosel
Part of an iron where the shaft meets the clubhead.

In-to-out path
The clubhead swings to the right of the target through the hitting area.

Lay-up
A shot played deliberately, or by necessity, short of the green.

Leading edge
The bottom, leading edge of the clubhead on an iron.

Lie
The location of the golf ball.

Loft
The angle at which the clubface sits, relative to perpendicular, and which in part determines the trajectory of the golf ball.

Open clubface
The clubface is aimed to the right of the target.

Open stance
The golfer's set-up is aligned to the left of the target.

Out-to-in path
The clubhead swings to the left of the target through the hitting area.

Posture
A word used to describe the overall body angles at address, as in "good posture" or "bad posture".

Set-up
An alternative description for a golfer's address position.

Slice
A shot that moves, severely, on a left-to-right trajectory through the air.

Stance
The process of standing to the ball in readiness to hit a shot, as in "taking your stance".

Swing path
The direction the club is swung, relative to the target line.

Sweet spot
The centre and optimum hitting area of the clubhead.

Target line
The imaginary line from the golf ball to the target.

Weight-shift
The process of transferring your weight from one foot to the other during the swing.

Index